Instant Vortex Plus Air Oven Cookbook 2023

1800 Days Super-Yummy & Healthy Air Fryer Oven

Recipes For Homemade Meals

Leigh M. Lee

CONTENTS

Breakfast Recipes

Classic Banana Beignets

Servings: 4
Cooking Time: 15 Minutes
Ingredients:

- 2 large ripe bananas
- 1 teaspoon vanilla essence
- 1/2 teaspoon cinnamon powder
- 1/2 teaspoon ground cloves
- 4 tablespoons brown sugar
- A pinch of kosher salt
- 1 cup all-purpose flour

Directions:

1. Select the "Air Fry" function and adjust the temperature to 360 degrees F. Press the "Start" key.
2. Line a baking pan with parchment paper and set it aside.
3. In a mixing bowl, thoroughly combine all the ingredients. Shape the mixture into equal balls and place them on the prepared baking pan.
4. Cook your beignets for about 10 minutes, flipping them halfway through the cooking time
5. Bon appétit!

Nutrition:

- Info205 Calories,0.5g Fat,45.7g Carbs,3.8g Protei.

Traditional Greek Tiganites

Servings: 5
Cooking Time: 15 Minutes
Ingredients:

- 1 ½ cups all-purpose flour
- 1 teaspoon baking powder
- 1/2 baking soda
- 1/2 teaspoon kosher salt
- 1 teaspoon granulated sugar
- 1 cup lukewarm water
- 1/2 cup Greek-style yogurt
- 1 large egg, whisked
- Topping:
- 1/2 cup honey

Directions:

1. In a mixing bowl, thoroughly combine the dry ingredients. In another bowl, whisk the wet ingredients. Add the wet mixture to the dry ingredients, and mix to combine well.

2. Grease a baking pan with nonstick cooking oil and set it aside.
3. Select the "Air Fry" function and adjust the temperature to 350 degrees F. Press the "Start" key.
4. Cook your tiganites for about 13 minutes or until they turn golden brown; work in batches, if needed. Enjoy!

Nutrition:

- Info222 Calories,1.3g Fat,47.3g Carbs,5.2g Protei.

Cinnamon Biscuit Donuts

Servings: 4
Cooking Time: 20 Minutes
Ingredients:

- 8 ounces refrigerated buttermilk biscuits
- 2 tablespoons butter, unsalted and melted
- 1/4 teaspoon grated nutmeg
- 1 teaspoon cinnamon powder
- 4 tablespoons powdered sugar

Directions:

1. Separate the biscuits and cut holes out of the center of each biscuit using a 1-inch round biscuit cutter; place them on parchment paper. Brush them with melted butter.
2. Select the "Air Fry" function and adjust the temperature to 350 degrees F. Press the "Start" key.
3. Lower your biscuits into the baking pan.
4. Air fry your biscuits at 340 degrees F for about 15 minutes or until golden brown, flipping them halfway through the cooking time.
5. Mix the nutmeg, cinnamon, and powdered sugar.
6. Roll the warm donuts onto the cinnamon sugar until well-coated on all sides. Bon appétit!

Nutrition:

- Info257 Calories,8.7g Fat,40g Carbs,4.5g Protei.

Breakfast German Kartoffelpuffer

Servings: 4
Cooking Time: 25 Minutes
Ingredients:

- 1 tablespoon olive oil
- 1 pound potatoes, peeled and grated
- 1 small shallot, chopped
- 1/2 teaspoon garlic powder
- Kosher salt and ground black pepper, to taste
- 2 large eggs, whisked
- 1 cup applesauce

Directions:

1. Grease a baking pan with olive oil and set it aside.
2. In a mixing bowl, thoroughly combine grated potatoes, shallot, garlic powder, salt, black pepper, and eggs; mix to combine well.
3. Now, spoon the batter into the prepared pan. Gently shake the pan to make sure that the batter is evenly spread.
4. Select the "Air Fry" function and adjust the temperature to 350 degrees F. Press the "Start" key. When the display indicates "Add Food", place the baking pan on the air fryer tray.
5. Cook the potato cake for about 20 minutes. Cut the potato cake into equal squares and serve warm with applesauce. Enjoy!

Nutrition:

- Info186 Calories,5.9g Fat,28.6g Carbs,5.9g Protei.

Old-fashioned Donuts

Servings: 6
Cooking Time: 15 Minutes
Ingredients:

- 2 cups all-purpose flour
- 1/2 cup milk
- 2 teaspoons active dry yeast
- 2 tablespoons granulated sugar
- 1/2 teaspoon kosher salt
- 1 egg, whisked
- 1/4 cup butter, melted
- 1 cup powdered sugar

Directions:

1. Select the "Air Fry" function and adjust the temperature to 360 degrees F. Press the "Start" key.
2. Mix all the ingredients, except for the powdered sugar, until a smooth and elastic dough forms.
3. Cover your dough with plastic wrap and allow it to rise in a warm place until doubled.
4. Drop spoonfuls of the batter onto the greased baking pan. Air Fry your donuts at 360 degrees F for 15 minutes or until golden brown, flipping them halfway through the cooking time.
5. Repeat with the remaining batter. Dust warm donuts with powdered sugar. Bon appétit!

Nutrition:

- Info319 Calories,9.4g Fat,52.1g Carbs,5.9g Protei.

Giant Dutch Pancake

Servings: 4
Cooking Time: 15 Minutes
Ingredients:

- 1 tablespoon butter
- 1 cup all-purpose flour
- 1/2 teaspoon kosher salt
- 1 teaspoon granulated sugar
- 2 eggs
- 1 cup milk
- 2 ounces cream cheese
- 1 large apple, cored and thinly sliced
- 1 teaspoon cinnamon powder

Directions:

1. Grease a baking pan with melted butter and set it aside.
2. In a mixing bowl, thoroughly combine the flour, salt, and sugar. Add in the eggs and milk; mix to combine well.
3. Now, spoon the batter onto the prepared pan. Gently shake the pan to make sure that the batter is evenly spread.
4. Select the "Air Fry" function and adjust the temperature to 350 degrees F. Press the "Start" key. When the display indicates "Add Food", place the baking pan on the air fryer tray.
5. Cook your pancake for about 13 minutes. Cut the pancake into equal squares and serve warm with cream cheese, apple, and cinnamon. Enjoy!

Nutrition:

- Info282 Calories,11.3g Fat,36.3g Carbs,9.2g Protei.

Spanish-style Cheese Sandwich

Servings: 1
Cooking Time: 10 Minutes
Ingredients:

- 2 pieces of bread
- 2 slices of cheddar cheese
- 1 tablespoon butter
- 1 teaspoon paprika

Directions:

1. Assemble your sandwich with cheese, butter, and paprika; you can use a toothpick to keep the sandwich together.
2. When the display indicates "Add Food", place the sandwich on the air fryer tray.
3. Select the "Toast" function and press the "Start" key.
4. Toast the sandwich for about 3 minutes or so. Serve immediately.

Nutrition:

- Info343 Calories,18.1g Fat,32.2g Carbs,14.1g Protei.

Sweet Corn Muffins

Servings: 6
Cooking Time: 15 Minutes
Ingredients:

- 1 cup flour
- 1 cup yellow cornmeal
- 1/2 teaspoon salt
- 1 teaspoon baking powder
- 1 teaspoon baking soda
- 1 cup buttermilk
- 1/4 cup water
- 2 large eggs
- 1/2 cup brown sugar
- 1/4 cup butter, melted

Directions:

1. Select the "Bake" function and adjust the temperature to 330 degrees F. Press the "Start" key.
2. In a mixing bowl, stir together the dry ingredients. Then, in a separate bowl, thoroughly combine all the wet ingredients.
3. Add the wet mixture to the dry ingredients and stir just until moistened. Spoon the batter into a parchment-lined muffin tin.
4. Bake your muffins for 13 minutes or until a tester comes out dry.
5. Bon appétit!

Nutrition:

- Info315 Calories,10.2g Fat,47g Carbs,7.6g Protei.

Spinach And Feta Baked Eggs

Servings: 2
Cooking Time: 15 Minutes
Ingredients:

- 2 teaspoons olive oil
- 4 large eggs
- 2 ounces feta cheese, crumbled
- 2 tablespoons fresh scallions, sliced
- 2 cups fresh baby spinach, torn into pieces
- 1 teaspoon dried rosemary
- 1 teaspoon dried parsley flakes
- 1 teaspoon dried basil
- Coarse sea salt and ground black pepper, to taste

Directions:

1. Select the "Bake" function and adjust the temperature to 350 degrees F and the time to 13 minutes. Press the "Start" key.
2. Meanwhile, brush two ramekins with olive oil. Then crack two eggs into each ramekin. Add in the remaining ingredients.
3. When the display indicates "Add Food", place the ramekins on the cooking tray in the center position.
4. Cook the eggs until set and serve warm. Enjoy!

Nutrition:

- Info277 Calories,20.2g Fat,5.8g Carbs,18.2g Protei.

Fried Bacon Slices

Servings: 4
Cooking Time: 15 Minutes
Ingredients:

- 8 slices of bacon

Directions:

1. Select the "Air Fry" function and adjust the temperature to 400 degrees F. Press the "Start" key.
2. When the display indicates "Add Food", place the bacon on the cooking tray. Cook for 10 minutes.
3. Bon appétit!

Nutrition:

- Info231 Calories,22.4g Fat,0.4g Carbs,7.2g Protei.

Traditional Indian Thalipith

Servings: 4
Cooking Time: 15 Minutes
Ingredients:
- 1 tablespoon ghee, melted
- 1/2 cup all-purpose flour
- 1/2 cup chickpea flour
- 1/2 cup rice flour
- A few dashes of hot sauce
- Sea salt and ground black pepper, to taste
- 1/2 teaspoon curry powder

Directions:
1. Grease a baking pan with melted ghee and set it aside.
2. In a mixing bowl, thoroughly combine the dry ingredients. In another bowl, whisk the wet ingredients. Add the wet mixture to the dry ingredients; mix to combine well.
3. Now, spoon the batter into the prepared pan. Gently shake the pan to make sure that the batter is evenly spread.
4. Select the "Air Fry" function and adjust the temperature to 350 degrees F. Press the "Start" key. When the display indicates "Add Food", place the baking pan on the air fryer tray.
5. Cook your thalipith for about 13 minutes. Cut the thalipith into equal squares and serve warm. Enjoy!

Nutrition:
- Info206 Calories,4.1g Fat,35.6g Carbs,5.6g Protei.

Baked Pita Bread

Servings: 2
Cooking Time: 10 Minutes
Ingredients:
- 2 pita breads
- 1 teaspoon Dijon mustard
- 2 ounces mozzarella cheese slices
- 1/2 teaspoon dried oregano
- 1 medium tomato, sliced
- 2 ounces Kalamata olives, pitted and sliced

Directions:
1. Assemble pita breads with the other ingredients; you can use a toothpick to secure your pitas.
2. Select the "Toast" function and press the "Start" key.
3. When the display indicates "Add Food", place the sandwich on the air fryer tray.
4. Toast the sandwich for about 3 minutes. Enjoy!

Nutrition:

- Info289 Calories,10.1g Fat,36g Carbs,13.7g Protei.

Greek-style Pita Pizza

Servings: 2
Cooking Time: 10 Minutes
Ingredients:
- 1 teaspoon olive oil
- 2 medium pita breads
- 4 tablespoons tomato sauce
- 4 ounces feta cheese, crumbled
- 1 tablespoon Greek seasoning mix

Directions:
1. Select the "Air Fry" function and adjust the temperature to 390 degrees F. Press the "Start" key.
2. Then, grease the cooking tray with olive oil.
3. Top your pita with tomato sauce, cheese, and seasoning mix.
4. Bake your pizza for about 5 minutes or until the cheese is melted. Bon appétit!

Nutrition:
- Info300 Calories,15.3g Fat,26.6g Carbs,11.7g Protei.

Mustard Cheese Sandwich

Servings: 2
Cooking Time: 10 Minutes
Ingredients:
- 4 large slices crusty bread
- 2 teaspoons Dijon mustard
- 4 ounces Colby cheese, thinly sliced
- 2 tablespoons chives, roughly chopped

Directions:
1. Assemble your sandwich with mustard, cheese, and chives; you can use a toothpick to keep the sandwich together.
2. Select the "Toast" function and press the "Start" key.
3. When the display indicates "Add Food", place the sandwich on the air fryer tray.
4. Toast the sandwich for about 3 minutes. Serve immediately.

Nutrition:
- Info385 Calories,20.4g Fat,31.5g Carbs,19.1g Protei.

Egg In A Hole

Servings: 2
Cooking Time: 10 Minutes

Ingredients:

- 4 slices bread
- 2 teaspoons butter
- 2 slices Colby cheese
- 2 eggs
- Kosher salt and freshly ground black pepper, to taste

Directions:

1. Select the "Air Fry" function and adjust the temperature to 380 degrees F. Press the "Start" key.
2. Use a sharp paring knife to scoop a circle in the middle of two slices of bread. Spread the butter on the other two slices of bread. Top them with cheese.
3. Top them with the bread slices with circles. Crack the eggs into the center of the bread; season with kosher salt and black pepper.
4. Place the bread with eggs on the air fryer tray.
5. Bake your bread at 380 degrees F for about 6 minutes. Serve immediately. Bon appétit!

Nutrition:

- Info315 Calories,18.3g Fat,20.3g Carbs,15.7g Protei.

Italian-style Crepes

Servings: 3
Cooking Time: 15 Minutes

Ingredients:

- 1 teaspoon coconut oil
- 1/2 cup all-purpose flour
- 1/2 teaspoon sea salt
- 1 tablespoon brown sugar
- 2 large eggs
- 1/2 cup milk

Directions:

1. Select the "Air Fry" function and adjust the temperature to 360 degrees F. Press the "Start" key.
2. Grease a baking pan with coconut oil and set it aside.
3. In a mixing bowl, thoroughly combine all the ingredients. Spoon the mixture into the prepared baking pan.
4. Cook your crepes for about 13 minutes or until cooked through.
5. Bon appétit!

Nutrition:

- Info177 Calories,6.2g Fat,20.7g Carbs,8.3g Protei.

Cheesy Egg Cups

Servings: 2
Cooking Time: 15 Minutes

Ingredients:

- 2 teaspoons olive oil
- 2 large egg
- 2 tablespoons sour cream
- 2 tablespoons cheddar cheese, grated
- Sea salt and ground black pepper, to taste

Directions:

1. Select the "Bake" function and adjust the temperature to 350 degrees F and the time to 13 minutes. Press the "Start" key.
2. Meanwhile, brush two silicone muffin cups with olive oil. Mix all the ingredients until well combined. Divide the mixture between the muffin cups.
3. When the display indicates "Add Food", place the muffin cups on the cooking tray in the center position.
4. Cook the egg cups to your desired texture, and serve warm. Enjoy!

Nutrition:

- Info277 Calories,20.2g Fat,5.8g Carbs,18.2g Protei.

Pigs In A Blanket

Servings: 6
Cooking Time: 10 Minutes

Ingredients:

- 6 ounces canned crescent rolls
- 1 tablespoon Dijon mustard
- 2 tablespoons butter, melted
- 12 mini cocktail sausage

Directions:

1. Line an air fryer tray with parchment paper.
2. Unroll the dough and separate into 4 triangles. Then, cut each triangle lengthwise into 3 triangles.
3. Spread each triangle with mustard and butter. Place one sausage on the shortest side of each triangle; roll them up.
4. When the display indicates "Add Food", place the rolls on the air fryer tray.
5. Bake your rolls for about 8 minutes. Bon appétit!

Nutrition:

- Info197 Calories,11.8g Fat,15.8g Carbs,5.5g Protei.

Easy Bacon Cups

Servings: 4
Cooking Time: 20 Minutes
Ingredients:
- 4 slices smoked bacon, sliced in half
- 4 thin slices tomato
- 4 eggs
- Sea salt and ground black pepper, to taste

Directions:
1. Select the "Air Fry" function and adjust the temperature to 370 degrees F. Press the "Start" key.
2. Put one slice of bacon and one slice of tomato in each muffin cup. Crack one egg on top of the tomato.
3. Sprinkle with sea salt and ground black pepper.
4. Bake in the preheated air fryer Oven for about 18 minutes. Bon appétit!

Nutrition:
- Info177 Calories,14.4g Fat,1.2g Carbs,8.9g Protei.

Classic Breakfast Cups With Pesto

Servings: 2
Cooking Time: 20 Minutes
Ingredients:
- 4 eggs
- 2 ounces ham, diced
- 2 tablespoons yellow onion, chopped
- A few dashes of hot sauce
- 1 tablespoon pesto sauce
- Sea salt and ground black pepper, to taste
- 1/2 teaspoon garlic powder
- 2 ounces feta cheese, crumbled

Directions:
1. Select the "Bake" function and adjust the temperature to 350 degrees F. Press the "Start" key.
2. Line a cupcake tin with parchment paper. Mix all the ingredients until well combined. Divide the mixture between muffin cups.
3. When the display indicates "Add Food", place the muffin tin on the cooking tray.
4. Bake the breakfast cups in the preheated air fryer oven for 15 minutes. Bon appétit!

Nutrition:
- Info252 Calories,15.4g Fat,6.3g Carbs,20.7g Protei.

Classic Breakfast Pancakes

Servings: 4
Cooking Time: 15 Minutes
Ingredients:

- 1 cup all-purpose flour
- 2 teaspoons baking powder
- 1 teaspoon baking soda
- 1/2 teaspoon salt
- 1 teaspoon granulated sugar
- 1 cup milk
- 1 medium egg
- 2 tablespoons coconut oil, melted

Directions:
1. In a mixing bowl, thoroughly combine the dry ingredients. In another bowl, whisk the wet ingredients. Add the wet mixture to the dry ingredients, and mix to combine well.
2. Grease a baking pan with nonstick cooking oil and set it aside.
3. Select the "Air Fry" function and adjust the temperature to 350 degrees F. Press the "Start" key.
4. Cook your pancakes for about 13 minutes, working in batches, if needed. Enjoy!

Nutrition:
- Info227 Calories,10.1g Fat,27.3g Carbs,6.5g Protei.

Double Cheese Breakfast Casserole

Servings: 4
Cooking Time: 15 Minutes
Ingredients:
- 1 teaspoon olive oil
- 1/2 pound smoked sausage, crumbled
- 1 small onion, chopped
- 1 teaspoon garlic, pressed
- 1 bell pepper, chopped
- 6 eggs, beaten
- 1/2 cup cream cheese, crumbled
- 1/2 cup cheddar cheese, shredded

Directions:
1. Select the "Bake" function and adjust the temperature to 360 degrees F. Press the "Start" key.
2. Grease the sides and bottom of a baking pan with olive oil. Arrange sausage, onion, garlic, and peppers in the prepared baking pan.
3. Then, whisk the eggs and cream cheese until well combined. Pour the mixture into the baking pan.
4. When the display indicates "Add Food", place the baking pan on the cooking tray. Air fry your casserole for about 10 minutes.
5. Top your casserole with cheddar cheese and select the "Broil" function; broil for about 5 minutes longer or until the cheese is bubbly.
6. Bon appétit!

Nutrition:
- Info353 Calories,25.7g Fat,7.3g Carbs,22.8g Protei.

Classic Breakfast Frittata

Servings: 4
Cooking Time: 20 Minutes
Ingredients:

- 1 tablespoon olive oil
- 6 eggs
- 1 shallot, peeled and chopped
- 6 tablespoons sour cream
- 1 cup Monetary-Jack cheese, shredded
- 1/2 teaspoon cayenne pepper
- Coarse sea salt and ground black pepper, to taste

Directions:

1. Select the "Air Fry" function and adjust the temperature to 330 degrees F. Press the "Start" key.
2. Grease a baking pan with nonstick cooking oil and set it aside.
3. In a mixing bowl, thoroughly combine all the ingredients. Pour the mixture into the prepared baking pan.
4. Bake your frittata for 15 minutes or until a tester comes out dry and clean.
5. Bon appétit!

Nutrition:

- Info265 Calories,20.5g Fat,3.8g Carbs,16.1g Protei.

Peppery Breakfast Quiche

Servings: 3
Cooking Time: 20 Minutes
Ingredients:

- 1 tablespoon olive oil
- 5 large eggs
- 1 red bell pepper, seeded and diced
- 1 green bell pepper, seeded and diced
- 2 tablespoons scallions, sliced
- 4 ounces brown mushrooms, sliced
- 1 teaspoon paprika
- Sea salt and ground black pepper, to taste
- 1/4 cup cream cheese, at room temperature

Directions:

1. Select the "Air Fry" function and adjust the temperature to 330 degrees F. Press the "Start" key.
2. Grease a baking pan with olive oil and set it aside.
3. In a mixing bowl, thoroughly combine all the ingredients. Pour the mixture into the prepared baking pan.
4. Bake your frittata for 15 minutes or until a tester comes out dry and clean.
5. Bon appétit!

Nutrition:

- Info365 Calories,19.7g Fat,34.7g Carbs,17.8g Protei.

Vegetable And Sausage Frittata

Servings: 4
Cooking Time: 20 Minutes
Ingredients:

- 1 teaspoon olive oil
- 1/2 pound cooked breakfast sausage, crumbled
- 6 eggs, beaten
- 1/2 cup cheddar cheese, shredded
- 1 chili pepper, seeded and chopped
- 1 small red onion, chopped
- 1 teaspoon garlic, pressed
- Sea salt and ground black pepper, to taste
- 1 teaspoon paprika

Directions:

1. Select the "Air Fry" function and adjust the temperature to 330 degrees F. Press the "Start" key.
2. Grease a baking pan with olive oil and set it aside.
3. In a mixing bowl, thoroughly combine all the ingredients. Pour the mixture into the prepared baking pan.
4. Bake your frittata for 15 minutes or until a tester comes out dry and clean.
5. Bon appétit!

Nutrition:

- Info367 Calories,28.6g Fat,6.4g Carbs,19.1g Protei.

Italian-style Spring Frittata

Servings: 4
Cooking Time: 10 Minutes
Ingredients:

- 6 eggs, whisked
- 3 ounces mozzarella cheese, shredded
- 1 cup cherry tomatoes, halved
- 1 pound baby spinach
- 2 stalks spring onions, sliced

Directions:

1. Select the "Air Fry" function and adjust the temperature to 330 degrees F. Press the "Start" key.
2. Grease a baking pan with cooking oil and set it aside.
3. In a mixing bowl, thoroughly combine all the ingredients. Pour the mixture into the prepared baking pan.
4. Bake your frittata for 15 minutes or until a tester comes out dry and clean.
5. Bon appétit!

Nutrition:

- Info167 Calories,6.8g Fat,7.3g Carbs,18.7g Protei.

Corn And Zucchini Fritters

Servings: 4
Cooking Time: 15 Minutes
Ingredients:

- 1 teaspoon olive oil
- 1 pound zucchini, peeled and grated (and squeezed)
- 1 cup corn kernels, canned or frozen
- 1/4 cup cheddar cheese, grated
- 2 scallion stalks, sliced
- 2 cloves garlic, finely minced
- 2 tablespoons fresh cilantro
- Kosher salt and freshly ground black pepper, to taste
- 1 teaspoon dried oregano
- 2 eggs, beaten
- 1/4 cup corn flour
- 1/2 cup all-purpose flour
- 1 teaspoon baking powder

Directions:

1. Select the "Air Fry" function and adjust the temperature to 350 degrees F. Press the "Start" key.
2. Grease a baking pan with olive oil and set it aside.
3. In a mixing bowl, thoroughly combine the remaining ingredients. Shape the mixture into equal patties and place them on the prepared baking pan.
4. Cook the fritters for about 10 minutes turning them over halfway through the cooking time. Bon appétit!

Nutrition:

- Info259 Calories,10.1g Fat,31.5g Carbs,14.2g Protei.

Cheesy Omelet With Scallions

Servings: 4
Cooking Time: 20 Minutes
Ingredients:

- 8 medium eggs
- 1/2 cup half-and-half
- 2 scallion stalks, chopped
- 2 ounces cream cheese, at room temperature
- Sea salt and ground black pepper, to taste
- 2 ounces cheddar cheese, shredded

Directions:

1. Select the "Bake" function and adjust the temperature to 350 degrees F. Press the "Start" key.
2. In the meantime, whisk the eggs with half-and-half. Add in the scallions, cheese, salt, and black pepper.
3. Pour the mixture into a lightly oiled baking pan.

4. When the display indicates "Add Food", place the baking pan on the cooking tray. Air fry the omelet for 10 minutes.
5. Top your omelet with cheddar cheese and press the "Broil" function; broil for 5 minutes longer or until the cheese is bubbly.
6. Bon appétit!
Nutrition:

- Info237 Calories,14.3g Fat,9.3g Carbs,16.6g Protei.

Breakfast Buttermilk Biscuits

Servings: 4
Cooking Time: 10 Minutes
Ingredients:

- 8 ounces refrigerated buttermilk biscuits
- 2 teaspoons mustard
- 4 slices bacon, diced
- 4 ounces cheddar cheese, cut into ten 3/4-inch cubes
- 1 tablespoon butter, melted

Directions:

1. Select the "Air Fry" function and adjust the temperature to 350 degrees F. Press the "Start" key.
2. Meanwhile, separate the dough into 4 biscuits.
3. Then, separate each biscuit into 2 layers and press them into rounds.
4. Top them with mustard, bacon, and cheese. Gently stretch the biscuit over the filling, pressing and firmly sealing around the edges of the biscuit. Brush the biscuits with melted butter.
5. When the display indicates "Add Food", place the biscuits on a parchment-lined baking tray. Bake your biscuits for about 7 minutes.
6. Bon appétit!
Nutrition:

- Info367 Calories,22.1g Fat,31.2g Carbs,11.2g Protei.

Sausage And Egg Cups

Servings: 3
Cooking Time: 20 Minutes
Ingredients:

- 6 large eggs
- Sea salt and ground black pepper, to taste
- 1 medium tomato, chopped
- 1 pork sausage, chopped
- 1 bell pepper, chopped
- 2 ounces cheddar cheese, shredded

Directions:

1. Select the "Bake" function and adjust the temperature to 350 degrees F and the time to 15 minutes. Press the "Start" key.
2. Meanwhile, brush three silicone muffin cups with olive oil. Mix all the ingredients until well combined. Divide the mixture between the muffin cups.
3. When the display indicates "Add Food", place the muffin cups on the cooking tray.
4. Bake the egg cups until set. Bon appétit!

Nutrition:

- Info327 Calories,23.3g Fat,7.1g Carbs,21.2g Protei.

Appetizers And Snacks Recipes

Parmesan Cocktail Meatballs

Servings: 6
Cooking Time: 20 Minutes
Ingredients:

- 1 pound ground pork
- 1/2 pound ground beef
- 1 cup breadcrumbs
- 1/4 cup milk
- 4 cloves garlic, pressed or minced
- 2 eggs, beaten
- 1 cup Parmesan cheese, grated
- 1/4 cup parsley, chopped
- 1 small onion, chopped
- 1 teaspoon dried oregano
- 1 teaspoon cayenne pepper
- Sea salt and ground black pepper, to taste

Directions:

1. Select the "Air Fry" function and adjust the temperature to 380 degrees F. Press the "Start" key.
2. Place a sheet of parchment paper in the air fryer oven pan.
3. In a mixing bowl, thoroughly combine all the ingredients. Then, drop rounds of the mixture in a single layer onto the prepared pan using a small scoop.
4. Air fry the meatballs for 10 minutes.
5. Select the "Broil" function and cook your meatballs for a further 5 minutes or until cooked through.
6. Bon appétit!

Nutrition:

- Info398 Calories,27.4g Fat,8.6g Carbs,28g Protei.

Italian Cheese Sticks

Servings: 6
Cooking Time: 10 Minutes
Ingredients:

- 2 medium eggs
- 1 teaspoon Italian seasoning
- 1 cup Italian breadcrumbs
- 6 mozzarella sticks

Directions:

1. Select the "Air Fry" function and adjust the temperature to 390 degrees F. Press the "Start" key.
2. Place a sheet of parchment paper in the air fryer oven pan.
3. Whisk the eggs in a mixing bowl; then, add in the seasoning and breadcrumbs and mix to combine well.
4. Dip each mozzarella stick into the egg mixture.
5. Air fry your mozzarella sticks for 5 minutes; turn them over and continue to cook for a further 2 minutes or until they are golden brown and crispy.
6. Bon appétit!

Nutrition:

- Info118 Calories,6.4g Fat,5.3g Carbs,8.7g Protei.

Kid-friendly Cheese Bites

Servings: 5
Cooking Time: 15 Minutes
Ingredients:

- 2 eggs
- 1/3 cup almond flour
- 1/4 cup parmesan cheese grated
- 3 tablespoons mayonnaise
- 1 teaspoon cayenne pepper
- 1/2 teaspoon garlic powder
- 1 teaspoon Italian seasoning mix
- 5 cheese sticks

Directions:

1. Select the "Air Fry" function and adjust the temperature to 390 degrees F. Press the "Start" key.
2. Place a sheet of parchment paper in the air fryer oven pan.
3. Whisk the eggs in a mixing bowl; then, add in the almond flour, cheese, mayonnaise, and seasoning; mix to combine well.
4. Dip each cheese stick into the egg/flour mixture.
5. Air fry the cheese sticks for 5 minutes; turn them over and continue to cook for a further 2 minutes or until they are golden brown and crispy.
6. Bon appétit!

Nutrition:

- Info258 Calories,21.4g Fat,3.4g Carbs,11.9g Protei.

Montreal Chicken Drumettes

Servings: 6
Cooking Time: 25 Minutes
Ingredients:

- 2 pounds chicken drumettes
- 1 cup tomato sauce
- 2 tablespoons olive oil
- 1 teaspoon Montreal seasoning mix
- 1 tablespoon fresh basil, chopped
- 1 tablespoon fresh parsley, chopped
- 1 tablespoon fresh cilantro, chopped

Directions:

1. Select the "Air Fry" function and adjust the temperature to 375 degrees F. Press the "Start" key.
2. Place a sheet of parchment paper in the air fryer oven pan. Toss the chicken wings with the remaining ingredients.
3. Arrange the chicken wings in a single layer in the air fryer oven perforated pan.

4. Air fry the chicken wings for 10 minutes; turn them over and air fry for a further 10 minutes or until they are browned and crunchy.
5. Bon appétit!
Nutrition:

- Info257 Calories,8.7g Fat,9.4g Carbs,31.9g Protei.

Rosemary Potato Chips

Servings: 4
Cooking Time: 20 Minutes
Ingredients:

- 1 pound russet potatoes, sliced
- 2 teaspoons olive oil
- Coarse sea salt, to taste
- 1 tablespoon dried rosemary, chopped

Directions:

1. Toss the potato slices with the remaining ingredients.
2. Select the "Air Fry" function and adjust the temperature to 400 degrees F. Press the "Start" key.
3. Arrange the potato slices on the parchment-lined air fryer oven perforated pan.
4. Air fry the potato slices for 15 minutes or until golden-brown and crisp.
5. Bon appétit!
Nutrition:

- Info110 Calories,2.3g Fat,20.5g Carbs,2.4g Protei.

Red Beetroot Chips

Servings: 2
Cooking Time: 10 Minutes
Ingredients:

- 2 medium-size red beets, peeled and sliced
- 2 teaspoons olive oil
- 1/2 teaspoon mustard powder
- 1 teaspoon cayenne pepper
- Kosher salt and freshly ground black pepper, to taste

Directions:

1. Select the "Air Fry" function and adjust the temperature to 380 degrees F. Press the "Start" key.
2. Toss all the ingredients on the parchment-lined air fryer oven perforated pan.
3. Air fry the beetroot chips for 6 minutes or until crispy.
4. Enjoy!
Nutrition:

- Info79 Calories,4.8g Fat,8.4g Carbs,1.4g Protei.

Butter Roasted Almonds

Servings: 9
Cooking Time: 20 Minutes
Ingredients:
- 1 ½ cups raw almonds
- 2 teaspoons butter, softened
- Himalayan pink salt, to taste

Directions:
1. Select the "Air Fry" function and adjust the temperature to 320 degrees F. Press the "Start" key.
2. Toss all the ingredients on the parchment-lined air fryer oven perforated pan.
3. Air fry the almonds for 15 minutes until the almonds turn brown inside.
4. Enjoy!

Nutrition:
- Info145 Calories,12.7g Fat,5.1g Carbs,5.2g Protei.

Sausage Wonton Wraps

Servings: 6
Cooking Time: 15 Minutes
Ingredients:
- 1 pound smoked sausage, crumbled
- 2 scallion stalks, chopped
- 2 tablespoons fish sauce
- 1 teaspoon ginger-garlic paste
- 1 package wonton wrappers
- 1 egg
- 1 tablespoon olive oil

Directions:
1. In a mixing bowl, thoroughly combine crumbled sausage, scallions, fish sauce, and ginger-garlic paste.
2. Divide the mixture between wonton wrappers.
3. Whisk the egg with 1 tablespoon of olive oil and 1 tablespoon of water.
4. Fold the wonton in half. Bring up the 2 ends of the wonton and use the egg wash to stick them together. Pinch the edges and coat each wonton with egg wash.
5. Place the folded wontons on the air fryer oven perforated pan, making sure not to crowd them.
6. Select the "Air Fry" function and adjust the temperature to 380 degrees F. Press the "Start" key.
7. Air fry your wontons for 10 minutes or until they're lightly browned.
8. Bon appétit!

Nutrition:
- Info188 Calories,10.3g Fat,9g Carbs,14.6g Protei.

Savory Herb Walnuts

Servings: 9
Cooking Time: 20 Minutes
Ingredients:
- 2 cups raw walnuts
- 2 tablespoons olive oil
- 1 teaspoon dried thyme
- 1 teaspoon dried rosemary
- 2 tablespoons nutritional yeast
- Sea salt and cayenne pepper, to taste

Directions:
1. Select the "Air Fry" function and adjust the temperature to 320 degrees F. Press the "Start" key.
2. Toss all the ingredients on the parchment-lined air fryer oven perforated pan.
3. Air fry the walnuts for 15 minutes or until the walnuts turn golden-brown.
4. Enjoy!

Nutrition:
- Info181 Calories,17.5g Fat,4.4g Carbs,4.5g Protei.

Gorgonzola Paprika Drumettes

Servings: 5
Cooking Time: 25 Minutes
Ingredients:
- 2 pounds chicken drumettes
- 1 teaspoon smoked paprika
- Kosher salt and ground black pepper, to taste
- 1 teaspoon cayenne pepper
- 1 tablespoon ancho chile pepper
- 1 teaspoon onion powder
- 1 teaspoon garlic powder
- 1 tablespoon brown sugar
- 1 teaspoon mustard powder
- 2 tablespoons butter
- 2 ounces gorgonzola cheese, crumbled

Directions:
1. Select the "Air Fry" function and adjust the temperature to 375 degrees F. Press the "Start" key.
2. Place a sheet of parchment paper in the air fryer oven pan. Toss the chicken wings with the remaining ingredients.
3. Arrange the chicken wings in a single layer in the air fryer oven perforated pan.
4. Air fry the chicken wings for 10 minutes; turn them over and air fry for a further 10 minutes or until they are browned and crunchy.
5. Bon appétit!

Nutrition:
- Info303 Calories,12.4g Fat,6.5g Carbs,39.6g Protei.

Crunch-crunch Party Mix

Servings: 10
Cooking Time: 15 Minutes
Ingredients:

- 2 cups pretzel sticks
- 2 cups oat cereal
- 1 cup almonds
- 1 cup walnuts
- 1 cup pine nuts
- 1/2 cup butter, at room temperature
- 1 tablespoon brown sugar
- 1 teaspoon garlic powder
- 1 teaspoon smoked paprika
- Coarse sea salt, to taste

Directions:

1. Select the "Air Fry" function and adjust the temperature to 320 degrees F. Press the "Start" key.
2. Toss all the ingredients on the parchment-lined air fryer oven perforated pan.
3. Air fry the ingredients for 15 minutes until they are crispy and warmed through.
4. Allow the party mix to cool completely before serving. Store your party mix in an airtight container for up to 3 months. Enjoy!

Nutrition:

- Info463 Calories,34.1g Fat,34.2g Carbs,10.1g Protei.

Old-fashioned Pear Fritters

Servings: 4
Cooking Time: 15 Minutes
Ingredients:

- 2 large pears, cored and sliced
- 1 cup plain flour
- 1/2 cup granulated sugar
- 1 tablespoon baking powder
- 1/2 cup apple juice
- 2 large eggs, whisked
- 3 tablespoons butter, melted
- A pinch of kosher salt
- A pinch of grated nutmeg
- 1/2 teaspoon cinnamon
- 1 teaspoon vanilla

Directions:

1. Select the "Air Fry" function and adjust the temperature to 380 degrees F. Press the "Start" key.
2. Place a sheet of parchment paper in the air fryer oven pan. Thoroughly combine all the ingredients.

3. Form the mixture into equal patties and place them in a single layer in the air fryer oven perforated pan.
4. Air fry the patties for 10 minutes, turning them over halfway through.
5. Bon appétit!

Nutrition:

- Info357 Calories,11.5g Fat,57.4g Carbs,6.9g Protei.

Cheese Prawn Wontons

Servings: 4
Cooking Time: 15 Minutes
Ingredients:

- 6 ounces shrimp, peeled, deveined and chopped
- 4 ounces cream cheese, at room temperature
- 2 teaspoons sesame oil
- 2 tablespoons green olive, chopped
- 2 cloves garlic, minced
- 1 teaspoon Sriracha, optional
- Sea salt and ground black pepper, to taste
- 16 wonton wrappers
- 1 extra-large egg, well beaten with 1 tablespoon of water

Directions:

1. In a mixing bowl, thoroughly combine all the ingredients, except the wonton wrappers.
2. Divide the mixture between the wonton wrappers.
3. Fold each wonton in half. Bring up the 2 ends of the wonton and use the egg wash to stick them together. Pinch the edges and coat each wonton with egg wash.
4. Place the folded wontons on the air fryer oven perforated pan, making sure not to crowd them.
5. Select the "Air Fry" function and adjust the temperature to 380 degrees F. Press the "Start" key.
6. Air fry your wontons for 10 minutes or until they're lightly browned.
7. Bon appétit!

Nutrition:

- Info277 Calories,14.3g Fat,21.4g Carbs,15.6g Protei.

Honey Garlic Chicken Wings

Servings: 5
Cooking Time: 25 Minutes
Ingredients:

- 1 pound chicken wings
- 1/4 cup all-purpose flour
- Kosher salt and ground black pepper, to taste
- 2 teaspoons olive oil
- 1/4 cup honey
- 2 tablespoons soy sauce
- 2 garlic cloves, crushed
- 1 teaspoon red chili flakes
- 1/4 cup beer

Directions:

1. Pat the chicken wings dry. Mix the remaining ingredients until everything is well incorporated.
2. Select the "Air Fry" function and adjust the temperature to 375 degrees F. Press the "Start" key.
3. Place a sheet of parchment paper in the air fryer oven pan. Dip the chicken wings in the prepared batter.
4. Arrange the chicken wings in a single layer in the air fryer oven perforated pan.
5. Air fry the chicken wings for 10 minutes; turn them over and air fry for a further 10 minutes or until they are browned and crunchy.
6. Bon appétit!

Nutrition:

- Info258 Calories,8.4g Fat,22.3g Carbs,22.2g Protei.

Cheese Broccoli Dip

Servings: 8
Cooking Time: 15 Minutes
Ingredients:

- 1 pound broccoli florets
- 2 teaspoon olive oil
- 2 scallion stalks, chopped
- 1 garlic clove, minced
- 1/4 cup cilantro leaves, chopped
- 1 lime, squeezed
- Sea salt and ground black pepper, to taste
- 1/4 cup cream cheese

Directions:

1. Toss the broccoli florets with olive oil.
2. Select the "Air Fry" function and adjust the temperature to 400 degrees F. Press the "Start" key.
3. Arrange the broccoli florets on the air fryer oven perforated pan, making sure not to crowd them.

4. Air fry the broccoli florets for 6 minutes or until cooked through, tossing them once or twice during the cooking time.
5. Blend the roasted broccoli with the remaining ingredients until creamy and uniform.
6. Bon appétit!

Nutrition:

- Info69 Calories,3.9g Fat,3.7g Carbs,3.5g Protei.

Brussel Sprout Chips

Servings: 2
Cooking Time: 10 Minutes
Ingredients:

- 2 cups Brussel sprouts, trimmed and separated into leaves
- 2 teaspoons olive oil
- Coarse salt and red pepper flakes, to taste
- 1/2 teaspoon smoked paprika
- 1/2 teaspoon turmeric powder

Directions:

1. Select the "Air Fry" function and adjust the temperature to 380 degrees F. Press the "Start" key.
2. Toss all the ingredients on the parchment-lined air fryer oven perforated pan.
3. Air fry the Brussel sprouts for 6 minutes or until crispy.
4. Enjoy!

Nutrition:

- Info91 Calories,4.9g Fat,10.9g Carbs,3.4g Protei.

Balsamic Baby Carrots

Servings: 4
Cooking Time: 25 Minutes
Ingredients:

- 1 pound baby carrots
- 1 stick butter
- 3 tablespoons agave nectar
- 2 tablespoons balsamic vinegar
- Sea salt and cayenne pepper, to taste

Directions:

1. Toss all the ingredients in a mixing bowl.
2. Select the "Air Fry" function and adjust the temperature to 380 degrees F. Press the "Start" key.
3. Arrange your carrots on the parchment-lined air fryer oven perforated pan.
4. Air fry your carrots for 20 minutes or until tender and cooked through.
5. Bon appétit!

Nutrition:

- Info261 Calories,23.4g Fat,13.4g Carbs,1.4g Protei.

Smoky Carrot Dip

Servings: 7
Cooking Time: 25 Minutes
Ingredients:

- 1 ½ pounds carrots, trimmed and sliced
- 3 teaspoons olive oil
- 2 cloves garlic, minced
- 1 teaspoon lime zest
- 1 teaspoon lemon juice
- 1 teaspoon Dijon mustard
- Sea salt and ground black pepper, to taste
- 1/4 cup tahini
- 1/2 teaspoon ground cumin
- 1/2 teaspoon turmeric powder

Directions:

1. Toss the carrots with olive oil in a mixing bowl.
2. Select the "Air Fry" function and adjust the temperature to 380 degrees F. Press the "Start" key.
3. Arrange your carrots on the parchment-lined air fryer oven perforated pan.
4. Air fry your carrots for 20 minutes or until tender and cooked through. Blend the carrots with the remaining ingredients until creamy and uniform.
5. Bon appétit!

Nutrition:

- Info113 Calories,6.8g Fat,12.4g Carbs,2.6g Protei.

Spicy Potato Chips

Servings: 4
Cooking Time: 20 Minutes
Ingredients:

- 1 pound russet potatoes, peeled and sliced
- 2 teaspoons olive oil
- Sea salt and cayenne pepper, to taste
- 1 teaspoon ancho chili pepper flakes

Directions:

1. Toss the potato slices with the remaining ingredients.
2. Select the "Air Fry" function and adjust the temperature to 400 degrees F. Press the "Start" key.
3. Arrange the potato slices on the parchment-lined air fryer oven perforated pan.
4. Air fry the potato slices for 15 minutes or until golden-brown and crisp.
5. Bon appétit!

Nutrition:

- Info115 Calories,2.3g Fat,21.6g Carbs,2.6g Protei.

Shrimp Pot Stickers

Servings: 4
Cooking Time: 15 Minutes
Ingredients:

- 12 medium shrimp, peeled and chopped
- 1 teaspoon ginger-garlic paste
- 2 tablespoons cocktail sauce
- 4 tablespoons cream cheese, room temperature
- 1/2 teaspoon red pepper flakes, crushed
- 1 package wrappers
- 2 teaspoon olive oil

Directions:

1. In a mixing bowl, thoroughly combine the shrimp, ginger-garlic paste, cocktail sauce, cream cheese, and red pepper flakes.
2. Divide the mixture between wonton wrappers.
3. Fold the wonton in half. Bring up the 2 ends of the wonton to stick them together. Pinch the edges and brush each wonton with olive oil.
4. Place the folded wontons on the air fryer oven perforated pan, making sure not to crowd them.
5. Select the "Air Fry" function and adjust the temperature to 380 degrees F. Press the "Start" key.
6. Air fry your wontons for 10 minutes or until they're lightly browned.
7. Bon appétit!

Nutrition:

- Info392 Calories,8.8g Fat,50.5g Carbs,26.4g Protei.

Coconut Fried Banana

Servings: 2
Cooking Time: 15 Minutes
Ingredients:

- 2 medium bananas, sliced
- 1 tablespoon avocado oil
- 2 tablespoons coconut flakes

Directions:

1. Select the "Air Fry" function and adjust the temperature to 350 degrees F. Press the "Start" key.
2. Toss the banana with avocado oil. Place a sheet of parchment paper in the air fryer oven pan.
3. Air fry the banana slices for 5 minutes; turn them over and continue to cook for a further 2 minutes or until they are golden.
4. Toss the banana slices with coconut flakes. Bon appétit!

Nutrition:

- Info192 Calories,8.8g Fat,29.4g Carbs,1.5g Protei.

Cheesy Broccoli Tots

Servings: 4
Cooking Time: 15 Minutes
Ingredients:
- 1 pound broccoli, grated
- 1/2 cup cheddar cheese, shredded
- 1 tablespoon extra-virgin olive oil
- 1 egg
- 1/2 cup panko breadcrumbs
- 2 cloves garlic, minced
- Sea salt and freshly ground black pepper, to taste

Directions:
1. Select the "Air Fry" function and adjust the temperature to 390 degrees F. Press the "Start" key.
2. Place a sheet of parchment paper in the air fryer oven pan. Thoroughly combine all the ingredients.
3. Form the mixture into equal balls and place them in a single layer in the air fryer oven perforated pan.
4. Air fry the broccoli tots for 10 minutes, turning them over halfway through.
5. Bon appétit!

Nutrition:
- Info145 Calories,9.9g Fat,6.7g Carbs,8.9g Protei.

Turkey Scallion Meatballs

Servings: 6
Cooking Time: 20 Minutes
Ingredients:
- 1 pound ground turkey
- 1/2 pound ground pork
- 1/4 cup scallions, chopped
- 1/4 cup fresh parsley leaves, chopped
- 2 cloves garlic, minced
- 1 cup breadcrumbs
- 1/2 cup cream of celery soup
- 2 eggs, beaten
- 1/2 cup Pecorino Romano cheese, grated
- Sea salt and ground black pepper, to taste

Directions:
1. Select the "Air Fry" function and adjust the temperature to 380 degrees F. Press the "Start" key.
2. Place a sheet of parchment paper in the air fryer oven pan.
3. In a mixing bowl, thoroughly combine all the ingredients. Then, drop rounds of the mixture in a single layer onto the prepared pan using a small scoop.
4. Air fry the meatballs for 10 minutes.
5. Select the "Broil" function and cook your meatballs for a further 5 minutes or until cooked through.
6. Bon appétit!

Nutrition:
- Info304 Calories,18.2g Fat,7.2g Carbs,26.3g Protei.

Authentic Baba Ghanoush

Servings: 8
Cooking Time: 25 Minutes
Ingredients:
- 1 ½ pounds eggplant, diced
- 4 tablespoons olive oil
- 1 medium head of garlic
- 1 tablespoon fresh lemon juice
- 1 tablespoon lemon zest
- 1/4 cup tahini
- Coarse sea salt and ground pepper, to taste
- 1 teaspoon smoked paprika

Directions:
1. Toss the eggplant with 2 tablespoons of olive oil. Place the head of garlic on a square piece of aluminum foil; bring the foil up and around the garlic.
2. Select the "Air Fry" function and adjust the temperature to 380 degrees F. Press the "Start" key.
3. Arrange the eggplant and wrapped garlic on the parchment-lined air fryer oven perforated pan.
4. Air fry the eggplant and garlic for 20 minutes or until they are tender and cooked through. Once the garlic is cool, gently squeeze on each clove (it will pop out of its skin).
5. Transfer the eggplant and garlic to the bowl of your food processor; add in the remaining ingredients and blend until creamy and smooth.
6. Bon appétit!

Nutrition:
- Info135 Calories,11g Fat,8.7g Carbs,2.5g Protei.

Texas-style Fried Pickles

Servings: 4
Cooking Time: 15 Minutes
Ingredients:
- 1 large egg, beaten
- 1/2 cup all-purpose flour
- 1/2 teaspoon onion powder
- 1 teaspoon garlic powder
- Sea salt and freshly cracked black pepper, to season
- 2 large dill pickles, sliced into rounds

Directions:
1. Whisk the eggs in a shallow bowl; add in the flour and spices; mix to combine. Dredge your pickles into the egg mixture.
2. Select the "Air Fry" function and adjust the temperature to 390 degrees F. Press the "Start" key.
3. Arrange the pickle chip on the parchment-lined air fryer oven perforated pan.
4. Air fry the pickle chip for 6 minutes or until crispy and cooked through. Work in batches, if needed. Enjoy!

Nutrition:
- Info93 Calories,1.6g Fat,15.5g Carbs,3.9g Protei.

Spicy Avocado Fritters

Servings: 4
Cooking Time: 10 Minutes
Ingredients:
- 2 large eggs
- 1 cup seasoned breadcrumbs
- 1/2 cup parmesan cheese, grated
- Sea salt and ground black pepper, to taste
- A few dashes of hot sauce
- 2 avocados, peeled, pitted and cut into wedges
- 2 teaspoon peanut oil (or sesame oil)

Directions:
1. In a shallow bowl, whisk the eggs until frothy. Add in the seasoned breadcrumbs, cheese, salt, black pepper, and hot sauce.
2. Dredge the avocado wedges in the breadcrumb mixture. Brush the avocado wedges with peanut oil on all sides.
3. When the display indicates "Add Food", place the avocado wedges in the air fryer oven perforated pan. Air fry them at 400 degrees F for 6 minutes.
4. Enjoy!

Nutrition:
- Info303 Calories,23.4g Fat,17.6g Carbs,9.9g Protei.

Honey Apple Chips

Servings: 4
Cooking Time: 35 Minutes
Ingredients:
- 2 medium apples, cored and sliced
- 1 tablespoon coconut oil, melted
- 2 tablespoons honey
- 1/4 teaspoon grated nutmeg
- 1 teaspoon ground cinnamon

Directions:
1. Select the "Air Fry" function and adjust the temperature to 300 degrees F. Press the "Start" key.
2. Toss your apples with the remaining ingredients. Place a sheet of parchment paper in the air fryer oven pan.
3. Air fry the apple slices for 15 minutes; turn them over and continue to cook for a further 15 minutes or until they are golden-browned.
4. Bon appétit!

Nutrition:
- Info112 Calories,3.6g Fat,21.4g Carbs,0.5g Protei.

The Best Cheese Broccomole

Servings: 7
Cooking Time: 15 Minutes
Ingredients:
- 1 pound broccoli florets
- 2 teaspoons olive oil
- 6 ounces feta cheese, crumbled
- 1/4 cup cream of onion soup
- 1 teaspoon cayenne pepper
- 1 teaspoon garlic powder
- Kosher salt and freshly ground black pepper, to taste
- 1/2 cup Parmesan cheese, grated

Directions:
1. Toss the broccoli florets with olive oil.
2. Select the "Air Fry" function and adjust the temperature to 400 degrees F. Press the "Start" key.
3. Arrange the broccoli florets on the air fryer oven perforated pan, making sure not to crowd them.
4. Air fry the broccoli florets for 6 minutes or until cooked through, tossing them once or twice during the cooking time.
5. Blend the roasted broccoli with feta cheese, onion soup, and spices until creamy and uniform. Spoon the sauce into a lightly greased casserole dish.
6. Top the sauce with parmesan cheese and select the "Broil" function. Broil the sauce until the cheese melts.
7. Bon appétit!

Nutrition:
- Info134 Calories,8.9g Fat,7.2g Carbs,7.5g Protei.

Baked Pita Wedges

Servings: 4
Cooking Time: 10 Minutes
Ingredients:
- 4 small pitas, cut into triangles
- 2 tablespoons extra-virgin olive oil
- 1 teaspoon garlic powder
- 1 teaspoon dried oregano
- 1 teaspoon dried rosemary
- Coarse sea salt and ground black pepper, to season

Directions:
1. Select the "Air Fry" function and adjust the temperature to 330 degrees F. Press the "Start" key.
2. Place a sheet of parchment paper in the air fryer oven pan.
3. Toss the pita triangles with the remaining ingredients. Air fry the pita triangles for 6 minutes, turning them over halfway through.
4. Bon appétit!

Nutrition:
- Info138 Calories,7.5g Fat,16.1g Carbs,2.9g Protei.

Sticky Baby Carrots

Servings: 4
Cooking Time: 25 Minutes
Ingredients:

- 1 pound baby carrots
- 2 tablespoons unsalted butter
- 2 tablespoons honey
- 1 teaspoon fresh dill
- 1 teaspoon parsley flakes

Directions:

1. Toss all the ingredients in a mixing bowl.
2. Select the "Air Fry" function and adjust the temperature to 380 degrees F. Press the "Start" key.
3. Arrange your carrots on the parchment-lined air fryer oven perforated pan.
4. Air fry your carrots for 20 minutes or until tender and cooked through.
5. Bon appétit!

Nutrition:

- Info110 Calories,4g Fat,18.3g Carbs,1.8g Protei.

Vegetables And Side Dishes Recipes

Roasted Carrot Mash

Servings: 4
Cooking Time: 25 Minutes
Ingredients:

- 1 ½ pounds carrots, trimmed and sliced
- 2 tablespoons olive oil
- 2 tablespoons butter
- 1 teaspoon ground cumin
- 1/4 teaspoon dried dill weed
- Sea salt and ground black pepper, to season
- 1 teaspoon cayenne pepper
- 1/2 cup whole milk

Directions:

1. Toss the carrots with olive oil in a mixing bowl.
2. Select the "Air Fry" function and adjust the temperature to 380 degrees F. Press the "Start" key.
3. Arrange your carrots on the parchment-lined air fryer oven perforated pan.
4. Air fry your carrots for 20 minutes or until tender and cooked through. Mash the carrots with the remaining ingredients until creamy and uniform.
5. Bon appétit!

Nutrition:

- Info219 Calories,14.1g Fat,21.8g Carbs,2.9g Protei.

Parmesan Broccoli Bites

Servings: 4
Cooking Time: 10 Minutes
Ingredients:

- 1 pound broccoli florets
- 2 tablespoons olive oil
- 1 teaspoon fresh garlic, minced
- 1/2 teaspoon onion powder
- Kosher salt and freshly ground black pepper, to taste
- 2 ounces parmesan cheese, grated

Directions:

1. Toss all the ingredients in a mixing bowl.
2. Select the "Air Fry" function and adjust the temperature to 400 degrees F. Press the "Start" key.
3. Arrange the broccoli florets on the air fryer oven perforated pan, making sure not to crowd them.
4. Air fry the broccoli florets for 6 minutes or until cooked through, tossing them once or twice during the cooking time.
5. Bon appétit!

Nutrition:

- Info165 Calories,11.2g Fat,9.8g Carbs,7.3g Protei.

Herby Sticky Carrots

Servings: 4

Cooking Time: 25 Minutes

Ingredients:

- 1 pound carrots, trimmed and cut into 1-inch pieces
- 2 tablespoons butter, melted
- 2 tablespoons agave nectar
- A pinch of kosher salt
- A pinch of grated nutmeg
- 1/2 teaspoon garlic powder

Directions:

1. Toss all the ingredients in a mixing bowl.
2. Select the "Air Fry" function and adjust the temperature to 380 degrees F. Press the "Start" key.
3. Arrange your carrots on the parchment-lined air fryer oven perforated pan.
4. Air fry your carrots for 20 minutes or until tender and cooked through.
5. Bon appétit!

Nutrition:

- Info108 Calories,6g Fat,13.4g Carbs,1.2g Protei.

Italian-style Mushroom Patties

Servings: 4

Cooking Time: 15 Minutes

Ingredients:

- 1 pound Cremini mushrooms, chopped
- 1 small onion, chopped
- 2 garlic cloves, minced
- 1 bell pepper, chopped
- 2 tablespoons parsley, chopped
- 2 tablespoons cilantro, chopped
- 2 large eggs, beaten
- 1/2 cup breadcrumbs
- 1 tablespoon Italian seasoning mix
- 1 tablespoons soy sauce
- 2 teaspoon olive oil

Directions:

1. Select the "Air Fry" function and adjust the temperature to 390 degrees F. Press the "Start" key.
2. Place a sheet of parchment paper in the air fryer oven pan. Thoroughly combine all the ingredients.
3. Form the mixture into equal balls and place them in a single layer in the air fryer oven perforated pan.
4. Air fry the patties for 10 minutes, turning them over halfway through the cooking time.
5. Bon appétit!

Nutrition:

- Info139 Calories,5.7g Fat,13.4g Carbs,7.4g Protei.

Air Fried Peppers

Servings: 4

Cooking Time: 20 Minutes

Ingredients:

- 4 bell peppers, seeded and sliced
- 1 onion, sliced
- 2 tablespoons olive oil
- Kosher salt and ground black pepper, to taste
- 1 teaspoon cayenne pepper
- 1 teaspoon dried oregano
- 1 teaspoon dried basil

Directions:

1. Toss all the ingredients in a mixing bowl.
2. Select the "Air Fry" function and adjust the temperature to 400 degrees F. Press the "Start" key.
3. Arrange the peppers and onions on the air fryer oven perforated pan, making sure not to crowd them.
4. Air fry the peppers and onions for 15 minutes or until they're browned, shaking the pan once or twice during cooking.
5. Bon appétit!

Nutrition:

- Info119 Calories,7.2g Fat,13.5g Carbs,2.3g Protei.

Buttery Green Beans

Servings: 4

Cooking Time: 15 Minutes

Ingredients:

- 1 pound fresh green beans, trimmed
- 2 teaspoons butter, melted
- Sea salt and ground black pepper, to taste
- 1 teaspoon hot paprika
- 1/2 teaspoon onion powder
- 1/2 teaspoon garlic powder

Directions:

1. Toss the green beans with the other ingredients in a mixing bowl.
2. Select the "Air Fry" function and adjust the temperature to 400 degrees F. Press the "Start" key.
3. Arrange the green beans on the parchment-lined air fryer oven perforated pan.
4. Air fry the green beans for 10 minutes or until they achieve a light brown color.
5. Bon appétit!

Nutrition:

- Info68 Calories,2.2g Fat,9.8g Carbs,2.7g Protei.

Cheese-stuffed Mushrooms

Servings: 4
Cooking Time: 15 Minutes
Ingredients:

- 12 button mushrooms, washed
- 1 tablespoon olive oil
- 2 garlic cloves, minced
- 1/2 cup Parmesan cheese, grated
- 4 tablespoons tortilla chips, crushed
- Sea salt and ground black pepper, to taste
- 1/2 teaspoon mustard powder
- 1/2 teaspoon onion powder

Directions:

1. Pat the mushrooms dry and remove the stalks.
2. In a mixing bowl, thoroughly combine the remaining ingredients. Divide the filling between the prepared mushrooms.
3. Select the "Air Fry" function and adjust the temperature to 360 degrees F. Press the "Start" key.
4. Arrange the mushrooms on the air fryer oven perforated pan, making sure not to crowd them.
5. Air fry the mushrooms for 9 minutes or until cooked through.
6. Bon appétit!

Nutrition:

- Info239 Calories,9.8g Fat,29.4g Carbs,9.3g Protei.

Greek-style Eggplant

Servings: 4
Cooking Time: 20 Minutes
Ingredients:

- 1 ½ pounds eggplants, diced
- 1 teaspoon garlic, minced
- 1 teaspoon dried oregano
- 1 teaspoon dried basil
- 2 tablespoons extra-virgin olive oil
- 1 teaspoon paprika
- Coarse sea salt and ground black pepper, to taste

Directions:

1. Toss all the ingredients in a mixing bowl.
2. Select the "Air Fry" function and adjust the temperature to 390 degrees F. Press the "Start" key.
3. Arrange your eggplant on the parchment-lined air fryer oven perforated pan.
4. Roast the eggplant for 15 minutes or until tender and cooked through.
5. Bon appétit!

Nutrition:

- Info111 Calories,7.2g Fat,11.8g Carbs,2.1g Protei.

Lebanese Eggplant Salad

Servings: 4
Cooking Time: 20 Minutes
Ingredients:

- 1 pound eggplant, diced
- 1 teaspoon olive oil
- 1 cup cherry tomatoes, halved
- 1 small onion, chopped
- 2 cloves garlic, pressed
- 1/4 cup extra-virgin olive oil
- Coarse sea salt and ground black pepper, to taste
- 1/2 teaspoon cumin
- 1 teaspoon oregano
- 1 teaspoon sumac
- 4 ounces canned chickpeas, drained
- 1/4 cup almonds, slivered

Directions:

1. In a mixing bowl, toss the eggplant with 1 teaspoon of olive oil.
2. Select the "Air Fry" function and adjust the temperature to 390 degrees F. Press the "Start" key.
3. Arrange your eggplant on the parchment-lined air fryer oven perforated pan.
4. Roast the eggplant for 15 minutes or until tender and cooked through.
5. Bon appétit!

Nutrition:

- Info258 Calories,19.1g Fat,49.2g Carbs,19.5g Protei.

Mashed Sweet Potatoes

Servings: 4
Cooking Time: 35 Minutes
Ingredients:

- 1 ½ pounds sweet potatoes, peeled and halved
- 1 tablespoon olive oil
- 2 tablespoons butter
- 1 teaspoon red pepper flakes, crushed
- Kosher salt and ground black pepper, to taste

Directions:

1. Toss the sweet potatoes with olive oil in a mixing bowl.
2. Select the "Air Fry" function and adjust the temperature to 400 degrees F. Press the "Start" key.
3. Arrange your sweet potatoes on the parchment-lined air fryer oven perforated pan.
4. Roast your sweet potatoes for 30 minutes or until tender and cooked through. Mash the sweet potatoes with the remaining ingredients.
5. Bon appétit!

Nutrition:

- Info236 Calories,9.2g Fat,35.4g Carbs,2.9g Protei.

Beet Salad With Gruyere Cheese

Servings: 4
Cooking Time: 25 Minutes
Ingredients:

- 1 pound fresh beets, peeled and cut into 1-inch pieces cubes
- 2 tablespoons extra-virgin olive oil
- 2 tablespoons red wine vinegar
- 1/2 teaspoon cumin
- 1/2 teaspoon mustard seeds
- Kosher salt and ground black pepper, to taste
- 4 ounces Gruyere cheese, crumbled

Directions:

1. Toss all the ingredients in a mixing bowl, except for the cheese.
2. Select the "Air Fry" function and adjust the temperature to 400 degrees F. Press the "Start" key.
3. Arrange the beets on the air fryer oven perforated pan, making sure not to crowd them.
4. Air fry the beets for 20 minutes or until they're browned, shaking the pan once or twice during cooking.
5. Top the roasted beets with cheese and enjoy!

Nutrition:

- Info235 Calories,16.4g Fat,12.2g Carbs,10.6g Protei.

Roasted Buttery Eggplant

Servings: 4
Cooking Time: 25 Minutes
Ingredients:

- 1 pound eggplant, cut into 1 ½ -inch pieces
- 2 tablespoons butter, melted
- 1 tablespoon olive oil
- 1/2 teaspoon onion powder
- 1/4 teaspoon cumin, ground
- 1 teaspoon garlic powder
- 1/2 teaspoon ancho chile powder

Directions:

1. Toss all the ingredients in a mixing bowl.
2. Select the "Air Fry" function and adjust the temperature to 380 degrees F. Press the "Start" key.
3. Arrange eggplant pieces on the parchment-lined air fryer oven perforated pan.
4. Air fry the eggplant pieces for 20 minutes or until tender and cooked through.
5. Bon appétit!

Nutrition:

- Info115 Calories,9.3g Fat,7.6g Carbs,1.4g Protei.

Roasted Baby Potatoes

Servings: 4
Cooking Time: 35 Minutes
Ingredients:

- 1 ½ pounds baby potatoes, scrubbed and halved
- 1 tablespoon fresh lemon juice
- 2 tablespoons olive oil
- 1 teaspoon garlic powder
- 1 teaspoon onion powder
- 1 teaspoon Italian seasoning mix
- Kosher salt and ground black pepper, to taste

Directions:

1. Toss the baby potatoes with the remaining ingredients in a mixing bowl.
2. Select the "Air Fry" function and adjust the temperature to 400 degrees F. Press the "Start" key.
3. Arrange the baby potatoes on the parchment-lined air fryer oven perforated pan. Bake the baby potatoes for 30 minutes, turning them over halfway through.
4. Bon appétit!

Nutrition:

- Info188 Calories,7.1g Fat,28.7g Carbs,3.6g Protei.

Italian Sausage Zucchini Boats

Servings: 4
Cooking Time: 20 Minutes
Ingredients:

- 1 pound zucchini
- 1 teaspoon dried Italian seasoning
- Sea salt and ground black pepper, to taste
- 2 tablespoons olive oil
- 1/2 pound Italian sausage, casings removed and crumbled
- 1 small onion, chopped
- 2 garlic cloves, minced
- 1 cup marinara sauce
- 1/2 cup mozzarella cheese, shredded

Directions:

1. Cut the zucchini into halves lengthwise. Scoop the flesh out of the zucchinis, using a spoon.
2. Mix all the ingredients, except for the mozzarella cheese.
3. Select the "Air Fry" function and adjust the temperature to 400 degrees F. Press the "Start" key.
4. Stuff your zucchini with the filling and place them on the parchment-lined air fryer oven perforated pan.
5. Roast the zucchini for 10 minutes or until tender. Select the "Broil" function and continue to bake for a further 5 minutes or until the cheese melts.
6. Bon appétit!

Nutrition:

- Info333 Calories,22.7g Fat,14.4g Carbs,19.5g Protei.

Parmesan Brussels Sprouts

Servings: 4
Cooking Time: 15 Minutes
Ingredients:
- 1 ½ pounds Brussels sprouts, trimmed and halved
- 3 tablespoons olive oil
- Sea salt and freshly ground black pepper, to taste
- 1 teaspoon lemon zest
- 1/2 cup Parmesan cheese, grated
- 2 tablespoons fresh parsley leaves, roughly chopped

Directions:
1. Toss the Brussels sprouts with olive oil, salt, black pepper, and lemon zest in a mixing bowl.
2. Select the "Air Fry" function and adjust the temperature to 375 degrees F. Press the "Start" key.
3. Arrange the Brussels sprouts on the parchment-lined air fryer oven perforated pan. Bake the Brussels sprouts for 5 minutes.
4. Select the "Air Fry" function and top your Brussels sprouts with cheese and parsley; continue to bake for a further 8 minutes or until the cheese melts.
5. Bon appétit!

Nutrition:
- Info201 Calories,10.5g Fat,16.4g Carbs,12.2g Protei.

Roasted Pepper And Cheese Bowl

Servings: 4
Cooking Time: 20 Minutes
Ingredients:
- 4 large bell peppers
- 2 tablespoons of olive oil
- Sea salt and ground black pepper, to taste
- 1 teaspoon garlic, minced
- 1 teaspoon dill weed
- 1 teaspoon Dijon mustard
- 2 tablespoons lemon juice
- 2 ounces feta cheese, crumbled

Directions:
1. Toss all the ingredients in a mixing bowl.
2. Select the "Air Fry" function and adjust the temperature to 400 degrees F. Press the "Start" key.
3. Arrange the peppers on the air fryer oven perforated pan, making sure not to crowd them.
4. Air fry the peppers for 15 minutes or until they're browned, shaking the pan once or twice during cooking.
5. Toss the peppers with the other ingredients. Bon appétit!

Nutrition:
- Info139 Calories,10.1g Fat,10.4g Carbs,3.8g Protei.

Italian-style Croquettes

Servings: 4
Cooking Time: 15 Minutes
Ingredients:
- 1 pound cauliflower, grated
- 1 small onion, chopped
- 2 garlic cloves, minced
- 2 tablespoons olive oil
- 1/2 tsp Italian seasoning
- 1 cup mozzarella cheese
- 1 large egg, beaten
- 1/2 cup all-purpose flour
- Kosher salt and ground black pepper, to taste

Directions:
1. Select the "Air Fry" function and adjust the temperature to 390 degrees F. Press the "Start" key.
2. Place a sheet of parchment paper in the air fryer oven pan. Thoroughly combine all the ingredients.
3. Form the mixture into equal balls and place them in a single layer in the air fryer oven perforated pan.
4. Air fry the croquettes for 10 minutes, turning them over halfway through.
5. Bon appétit!

Nutrition:
- Info212 Calories,8.4g Fat,20.9g Carbs,14.8g Protei.

Easy Roasted Asparagus

Servings: 4
Cooking Time: 10 Minutes
Ingredients:
- 1 ½ pounds asparagus, trimmed
- 2 tablespoons olive oil
- 1 teaspoon cayenne pepper
- 1 teaspoon granulated garlic (or garlic powder)
- 1 teaspoon grated lemon zest
- Kosher salt and freshly cracked black pepper, to taste

Directions:
1. Toss all the ingredients in a mixing bowl.
2. Select the "Air Fry" function and adjust the temperature to 400 degrees F. Press the "Start" key.
3. Arrange the asparagus spears on the air fryer oven perforated pan, making sure not to crowd them.
4. Air fry the asparagus for 8 minutes or until tender and bright green, tossing halfway through the cooking time.
5. Bon appétit!

Nutrition:
- Info96 Calories,7g Fat,7.2g Carbs,3.8g Protei.

Ritzy Stuffed Mushrooms

Servings: 4
Cooking Time: 20 Minutes

Ingredients:

- 1 pound button mushrooms, stalks removed
- 1/2 cup crackers, crushed
- 2 cloves garlic, minced
- 2 tablespoons butter, softened
- Kosher salt and freshly ground black pepper, to taste
- 1/4 cup Pecorino cheese, grated
- 2 tablespoons fresh parsley, chopped
- 2 tablespoons fresh cilantro, chopped

Directions:

1. Pat the mushrooms dry. Toss the remaining ingredients in a mixing bowl.
2. Divide the filling between the prepared mushrooms.
3. Select the "Air Fry" function and adjust the temperature to 350 degrees F. Press the "Start" key.
4. Arrange the mushrooms on the parchment-lined air fryer oven perforated pan. Bake the mushrooms for 12 minutes or until tender and cooked through.
5. Bon appétit!

Nutrition:

- Info148 Calories,10.6g Fat,8.3g Carbs,6.1g Protei.

Parmesan Zucchini Tots

Servings: 4
Cooking Time: 15 Minutes

Ingredients:

- 1 pound zucchini, grated
- 4 tablespoons almond flour
- 1 teaspoon Italian seasoning mix
- 1 large egg, whisked
- 1/2 cup parmesan cheese, shredded
- 1 cup breadcrumbs

Directions:

1. Select the "Air Fry" function and adjust the temperature to 390 degrees F. Press the "Start" key.
2. Place a sheet of parchment paper in the air fryer oven pan. Thoroughly combine all the ingredients.
3. Form the mixture into equal balls and place them in a single layer in the air fryer oven perforated pan.
4. Air fry the zucchini tots for 10 minutes, turning them over halfway through.
5. Bon appétit!

Nutrition:

- Info192 Calories,11.1g Fat,13.6g Carbs,25.9g Protei.

Herbed Roasted Zucchini

Servings: 4
Cooking Time: 20 Minutes

Ingredients:

- 1 pound zucchini, quartered lengthwise
- 1 tablespoon Italian seasoning
- Coarse sea salt and ground black pepper, to taste
- 4 tablespoons extra-virgin olive oil
- 2 tablespoons freshly squeezed lemon juice
- 1 teaspoon Dijon mustard
- 2 tablespoons fresh parsley, chopped
- 2 tablespoons fresh basil, chopped
- 1 tablespoon fresh mint, chopped

Directions:

1. Toss all the ingredients in a mixing bowl.
2. Select the "Air Fry" function and adjust the temperature to 400 degrees F. Press the "Start" key.
3. Arrange the zucchini on the parchment-lined air fryer oven perforated pan.
4. Roast the zucchini for 15 minutes or until tender and cooked through.
5. Bon appétit!

Nutrition:

- Info158 Calories,14.6g Fat,6.6g Carbs,2.1g Protei.

Moroccan Carrot Salad

Servings: 4
Cooking Time: 25 Minutes

Ingredients:

- 1 pound carrots, peeled and sliced
- 1 teaspoon olive oil
- 2 garlic cloves, minced
- 1/2 lemon, squeezed
- 1 teaspoon ground cumin
- 1/4 cup extra-virgin olive oil
- Sea salt and ground black pepper, to taste
- 2 cups baby spinach
- 1/4 cup dates, pitted and halved

Directions:

1. Toss the carrot with 1 teaspoon of olive oil.
2. Select the "Air Fry" function and adjust the temperature to 380 degrees F. Press the "Start" key.
3. Arrange your carrots on the parchment-lined air fryer oven perforated pan.
4. Air fry your carrots for 20 minutes or until cooked through. Toss the carrots with the remaining ingredients.
5. Bon appétit!

Nutrition:

- Info215 Calories,15.1g Fat,20.5g Carbs,2.2g Protei.

Roasted Fennel Salad

Servings: 4
Cooking Time: 20 Minutes
Ingredients:
- 1 pound fennel bulbs, quartered
- 1 shallot, sliced
- 4 cups lightly packed mixed greens
- 1 bell pepper, sliced
- 2 tablespoons pure maple syrup
- 1 tablespoon fresh lime juice
- 1 teaspoon Dijon mustard
- 2 tablespoons apple cider vinegar
- 3 cloves garlic, chopped
- 1/4 cup extra-virgin olive oil
- Kosher salt and freshly ground black pepper
- 1/4 cup pine nuts, toasted

Directions:
1. Select the "Air Fry" function and adjust the temperature to 370 degrees F. Press the "Start" key.
2. Arrange the fennel wedges on the parchment-lined air fryer oven perforated pan. Air fry the fennel wedges for 15 minutes or until tender.
3. Cut the fennel into small pieces and add in the other vegetables. In a small mixing bowl, whisk the maple syrup, lime juice, mustard, vinegar, garlic, olive oil, salt, and black pepper.
4. Dress the salad, garnish with toasted nuts, and serve immediately. Bon appétit!

Nutrition:
- Info318 Calories,21.3g Fat,30.5g Carbs,4.8g Protei.

Grandma's Roasted Squash

Servings: 4
Cooking Time: 15 Minutes
Ingredients:
- 1 pound butternut squash, cut into 1/2-inch chunks
- 2 tablespoons coconut oil
- 2 tablespoons pure maple syrup
- A pinch of kosher salt
- A pinch of grated nutmeg
- 1/2 teaspoon ground cinnamon
- 1/2 teaspoon ground cloves

Directions:
1. Toss all the ingredients in a mixing bowl.
2. Select the "Roast" function and adjust the temperature to 380 degrees F. Press the "Start" key.
3. Arrange your squash on the parchment-lined air fryer oven perforated pan.

4. Air fry your squash for 12 minutes or until tender and cooked through.
5. Bon appétit!
Nutrition:
- Info133 Calories,6.9g Fat,18.7g Carbs,0.9g Protei.

Cheesy Butternut Squash

Servings: 4
Cooking Time: 15 Minutes
Ingredients:
- 1 ½ pounds butternut squash, cut into 1/2-inch chunks
- 2 tablespoons extra-virgin olive oil
- 1 teaspoon lemon zest
- A pinch of grated nutmeg
- Kosher salt and cayenne pepper, to taste
- 4 ounces Parmesan cheese, grated

Directions:
1. Toss all the ingredients in a mixing bowl.
2. Select the "Roast" function and adjust the temperature to 380 degrees F. Press the "Start" key.
3. Arrange your squash on the parchment-lined air fryer oven perforated pan.
4. Roast your squash for 12 minutes or until tender and cooked through.
5. Bon appétit!
Nutrition:
- Info260 Calories,14.6g Fat,24.4g Carbs,9.9g Protei.

French-style Roasted Parsnip

Servings: 4
Cooking Time: 25 Minutes
Ingredients:
- 1 ½ pounds parsnips, cut into 1/2-inch chunks
- 2 tablespoons extra-virgin olive oil
- 1 tablespoon Herbs de Province
- Kosher salt and cayenne pepper, to taste
- 2 tablespoons fresh parsley, chopped

Directions:
1. Toss all the ingredients in a mixing bowl.
2. Select the "Air Fry" function and adjust the temperature to 380 degrees F. Press the "Start" key.
3. Arrange your parsnips on the parchment-lined air fryer oven perforated pan.
4. Air fry your parsnips for 20 minutes or until tender and cooked through.
5. Bon appétit!
Nutrition:
- Info186 Calories,7.3g Fat,30.1g Carbs,2.5g Protei.

Roasted Sweet Potatoes

Servings: 4
Cooking Time: 40 Minutes
Ingredients:

- 1 pound sweet potatoes, peeled and diced
- 2 teaspoons olive oil
- 1 teaspoon cayenne pepper
- 1/2 teaspoon dried dill weed
- Sea salt and freshly ground black pepper, to taste

Directions:

1. Toss all the ingredients in a mixing bowl.
2. Select the "Roast" function and adjust the temperature to 380 degrees F. Press the "Start" key.
3. Arrange your sweet potatoes on the parchment-lined air fryer oven perforated pan.
4. Roast your sweet potatoes for 35 minutes or until tender and cooked through.
5. Bon appétit!

Nutrition:

- Info119 Calories,2.3g Fat,23.1g Carbs,1.9g Protei.

Beet, Apple And Cranberry Salad

Servings: 4
Cooking Time: 25 Minutes
Ingredients:

- 1 pound beets, peeled and cut into bite-sized pieces
- 2 teaspoons olive oil
- 4 cups baby spinach
- 1 apple, cored and diced
- 1/2 cup dried cranberries
- Vinaigrette:
- 1/3 cup extra-virgin olive oil
- 3 tablespoons apple cider vinegar
- 1 teaspoon yellow mustard
- 2 garlic cloves, minced
- Kosher salt and ground black pepper, to taste

Directions:

1. Toss the beets with olive oil until well coated.
2. Select the "Air Fry" function and adjust the temperature to 400 degrees F. Press the "Start" key.
3. Arrange the beets on the air fryer oven perforated pan. Air fry the beets for 20 minutes, shaking the pan once or twice during cooking.
4. Toss the roasted beets with the remaining ingredients and enjoy!

Nutrition:

- Info281 Calories,20.6g Fat,23.1g Carbs,2.8g Protei.

Buttery Roasted Carrots

Servings: 4
Cooking Time: 25 Minutes
Ingredients:

- 1 pound carrots, sliced lengthwise
- 2 teaspoons butter, melted
- 1 teaspoon cayenne pepper
- 1 teaspoon dried oregano
- Kosher salt and ground black pepper, to taste

Directions:

1. Toss all the ingredients in a mixing bowl.
2. Select the "Air Fry" function and adjust the temperature to 380 degrees F. Press the "Start" key.
3. Arrange your carrots on the parchment-lined air fryer oven perforated pan.
4. Air fry your carrots for 20 minutes or until tender and cooked through.
5. Bon appétit!

Nutrition:

- Info66 Calories,2.4g Fat,11.2g Carbs,1.6g Protei.

Dijon Feta Broccoli

Servings: 4
Cooking Time: 10 Minutes
Ingredients:

- 1 pound broccoli florets
- 1 teaspoon lemon zest, grated
- 2 tablespoons butter, melted
- 2 garlic cloves, minced
- 1 teaspoon Dijon mustard
- 2 ounces feta cheese crumbled
- Sea salt and ground black pepper, to taste

Directions:

1. Toss all the ingredients in a mixing bowl.
2. Select the "Air Fry" function and adjust the temperature to 400 degrees F. Press the "Start" key.
3. Arrange the broccoli florets on the air fryer oven perforated pan, making sure not to crowd them.
4. Air fry the broccoli florets for 6 minutes or until cooked through, tossing them once or twice during the cooking time.
5. Bon appétit!

Nutrition:

- Info118 Calories,9.3g Fat,4.5g Carbs,5.8g Protei.

Vegan Recipes

Asian-style Brussels Sprouts

Servings: 4
Cooking Time: 20 Minutes
Ingredients:
- 1 ½ pounds Brussels sprouts, trimmed and halved
- 2 teaspoons sesame oil
- 1 teaspoon Five-spice powder
- 1 teaspoon red pepper flakes, crushed
- Kosher salt and ground black pepper, to taste
- 2 tablespoons balsamic vinegar
- 2 teaspoons agave nectar

Directions:
1. Toss the Brussels sprouts with the remaining ingredients in a mixing bowl.
2. Select the "Air Fry" function and adjust the temperature to 375 degrees F. Press the "Start" key.
3. Arrange the Brussels sprouts on the parchment-lined air fryer oven perforated pan. Bake the Brussels sprouts for 5 minutes.
4. Increase the heat to 400 degrees F. Give the pan a good shake and continue to cook for another 8 minutes or until tender.
5. Bon appétit!

Nutrition:
- Info110 Calories,2.8g Fat,18.6g Carbs,6.1g Protei.

Avocado And Corn Fritters

Servings: 4
Cooking Time: 15 Minutes
Ingredients:
- 1 large avocado, pitted, peeled and chopped
- 4 tablespoons creamed corn kernels
- 3 tablespoons soy yogurt
- 1/4 cup all-purpose flour
- Sea salt and ground black pepper, to taste
- 2 tablespoons vegan mayonnaise

Directions:
1. Select the "Air Fry" function and adjust the temperature to 360 degrees F. Press the "Start" key.
2. Grease a baking pan with nonstick cooking oil.
3. In a mixing bowl, thoroughly combine all the ingredients. Shape the mixture into equal patties and place them on the prepared baking pan.
4. Cook the fritters for about 12 minutes, turning them over halfway through the cooking time. Bon appétit!

Nutrition:
- Info184 Calories,13.1g Fat,15.2g Carbs,4g Protei.

Broccoli With Pine Nuts

Servings: 4
Cooking Time: 15 Minutes
Ingredients:
- 1 pound broccoli florets
- 2 tablespoons olive oil
- 1 teaspoon garlic powder
- 1/2 teaspoon cumin powder
- 1/2 teaspoon ground bay leaf
- Sea salt and ground black pepper, to taste
- 2 tablespoons nutritional yeast
- 2 tablespoons pine nuts

Directions:
1. Toss the broccoli florets with olive oil and spices.
2. Select the "Air Fry" function and adjust the temperature to 400 degrees F. Press the "Start" key.
3. Arrange the broccoli florets on the air fryer oven perforated pan, making sure not to crowd them.
4. Air fry the broccoli florets for 6 minutes or until cooked through, tossing them once or twice during cooking time.
5. Toss the broccoli florets with nutritional yeast and pine nuts.
6. Bon appétit!

Nutrition:
- Info157 Calories,10.7g Fat,11.8g Carbs,6.4g Protei.

Classic Fried Tofu

Servings: 4
Cooking Time: 30 Minutes
Ingredients:
- 1 block extra-firm tofu, pressed and cut into bite-sized cubes
- 2 teaspoons sesame oil
- 2 tablespoons soy sauce
- 1/2 teaspoon red pepper flakes, crushed
- 1 teaspoon ginger-garlic paste

Directions:
1. In a mixing bowl, thoroughly combine all the ingredients.
2. Select the "Air Fry" function and adjust the temperature to 395 degrees F. Press the "Start" key.
3. Arrange the tofu on the air fryer oven perforated pan, making sure not to crowd them.
4. Air fry the tofu cubes for 25 minutes or until golden brown; make sure to toss them occasionally to ensure even cooking.
5. Bon appétit!

Nutrition:
- Info147 Calories,10.9g Fat,4.4g Carbs,11.8g Protei.

Classic Lentil Meatballs

Servings: 4

Cooking Time: 20 Minutes

Ingredients:

- 2 cups red lentils, cooked and rinsed
- 1/2 cup whole-wheat flour
- 1/2 teaspoon baking powder
- 2 tablespoons walnuts, ground
- 1 tablespoon flaxseed, ground
- 2 teaspoons nutritional yeast
- 1 small onion, chopped
- 2 garlic cloves, pressed
- 1/4 cup tomato paste
- 2 tablespoons fresh parsley leaves, chopped
- 1 tablespoon fresh dill weed, chopped
- Sea salt and ground black pepper, to taste
- 1 teaspoon smoked paprika

Directions:

1. Select the "Air Fry" function and adjust the temperature to 400 degrees F. Press the "Start" key.

2. Place a sheet of parchment paper in the air fryer oven pan. Thoroughly combine all the ingredients.

3. Form the mixture into equal balls and place them in a single layer in the air fryer oven perforated pan.

4. Air fry the balls for 15 minutes or until cooked through. Serve hot and enjoy!

Nutrition:

- Info305 Calories,10.5g Fat,40.4g Carbs,17.1g Protei.

Fried Tofu With Sweet Potatoes

Servings: 5

Cooking Time: 35 Minutes

Ingredients:

- 1 pound sweet potatoes, peeled and cut into 1-inch chunks
- 10 ounces extra-firm tofu, pressed and cut into 1-inch chunks
- 1 teaspoon garlic, minced
- 2 tablespoons scallions, chopped
- 1 teaspoon paprika - divided
- Kosher salt and ground black pepper, to taste
- 2 tablespoons cornstarch
- 2 tablespoons olive oil

Directions:

1. In a mixing bowl, thoroughly combine all the ingredients.

2. Select the "Air Fry" function and adjust the temperature to 395 degrees F. Press the "Start" key.

3. Arrange the sweet potatoes on the air fryer oven perforated pan, making sure not to crowd them.

4. Air fry the sweet potatoes for 20 minutes or until soft; make sure to toss them occasionally to ensure even cooking.

5. Add in the tofu cubes and continue cooking for a further 10 minutes or until cooked through.

6. Bon appétit!

Nutrition:

- Info188 Calories,8.8g Fat,21.4g Carbs,7.7g Protei.

Mediterranean-style Fingerling Potatoes

Servings: 4

Cooking Time: 35 Minutes

Ingredients:

- 1 ½ pounds fingerling potatoes, scrubbed
- 2 tablespoons olive oil
- 1 teaspoon garlic powder
- 1 tablespoon fresh parsley, chopped
- 2 teaspoons fresh thyme, chopped
- 1 teaspoon red pepper flakes, crushed
- Sea salt and ground black pepper, to taste

Directions:

1. Toss the fingerling potatoes with the remaining ingredients in a mixing bowl.

2. Select the "Air Fry" function and adjust the temperature to 400 degrees F. Press the "Start" key.

3. Arrange the fingerling potatoes on the parchment-lined air fryer oven perforated pan. Bake the fingerling potatoes for 30 minutes, turning them over halfway through.

4. Bon appétit!

Nutrition:

- Info197 Calories,6.9g Fat,30.4g Carbs,3.6g Protei.

Spicy Red Potatoes

Servings: 4
Cooking Time: 40 Minutes
Ingredients:

- 1 ½ pounds red potatoes, peeled and cut into wedges
- 3 tablespoons olive oil
- 2 garlic cloves, pressed
- 1 teaspoon hot sauce
- Sea salt and ground black pepper, to taste

Directions:

1. Select the "Air Fry" function and adjust the temperature to 400 degrees F. Press the "Start" key.
2. Toss the potato wedges with the remaining ingredients.
3. When the display indicates "Add Food", place the potato wedges in the air fryer oven perforated pan.
4. Air fry the potato wedges for 35 minutes, turning them over at the halfway point.
5. Bon appétit!

Nutrition:

- Info217 Calories,10.4g Fat,28.7g Carbs,3.5g Protei.

Oatmeal Muffins With Veggies

Servings: 6
Cooking Time: 25 Minutes
Ingredients:

- 1 ½ cups rolled oats
- 1 cup oat milk (or rice milk)
- Sea salt and ground black pepper, to taste
- 2 tablespoons olive oil
- 1 cup broccoli, grated
- 1 red bell pepper, chopped
- 2 tablespoons scallions, chopped
- 1 teaspoon granulated garlic

Directions:

1. Select the "Air Fry" function and adjust the temperature to 390 degrees F. Press the "Start" key.
2. Thoroughly combine all the ingredients. Spoon the mixture into a greased muffin tin.
3. Air fry the oatmeal cups for 15 minutes or until golden brown.
4. Bon appétit!

Nutrition:

- Info229 Calories,8.6g Fat,30.4g Carbs,8.6g Protei.

Classic Cauliflower Steaks

Servings: 4
Cooking Time: 20 Minutes
Ingredients:

- 1 pound cauliflower, cut into 1 ½-inch thick steaks
- Sea salt and ground black pepper, to taste
- 1 teaspoon onion powder
- 1 teaspoon garlic powder
- 1 teaspoon cayenne pepper
- 1 teaspoon dried parsley flakes
- 2 tablespoons extra-virgin olive oil

Directions:

1. Toss the cauliflower steaks with the other ingredients.
2. Select the "Air Fry" function and adjust the temperature to 380 degrees F. Press the "Start" key.
3. When the display indicates "Add Food", place the cauliflower steaks in the air fryer oven perforated pan.
4. Cook the cauliflower for 10 minutes. Increase the temperature of the oven to 400 degrees F and continue to cook for 7 to 8 minutes more.
5. Serve warm and enjoy!

Nutrition:

- Info102 Calories,7.4g Fat,8g Carbs,2.6g Protei.

Crispy Breaded Mushrooms

Servings: 4
Cooking Time: 15 Minutes
Ingredients:

- 1 pound brown mushrooms
- 1/4 cup oat milk (or rice milk)
- 1 cup tortilla chips, crushed
- 2 teaspoon olive oil
- 2 garlic cloves, minced
- Sea salt and ground black pepper, to taste
- 1 teaspoon smoked paprika
- 2 tablespoons nutritional yeast

Directions:

1. Pat the mushrooms dry.
2. In a mixing bowl, thoroughly combine all the remaining ingredients. Then, dip the mushrooms in the breadcrumb mixture, coating them on all sides.
3. Select the "Air Fry" function and adjust the temperature to 360 degrees F. Press the "Start" key.
4. Arrange the mushrooms on the air fryer oven perforated pan, making sure not to crowd them. Air fry the mushrooms for 10 minutes or until golden brown.
5. Bon appétit!

Nutrition:

- Info243 Calories,10.7g Fat,30.1g Carbs,8.6g Protei.

Asian-style Tofu With Beans

Servings: 4
Cooking Time: 30 Minutes
Ingredients:

- 1 extra-firm tofu, cubed
- 1/2 teaspoon ginger, peeled and grated
- 2 tablespoons corn starch
- 1 teaspoon garlic powder
- 1/2 teaspoon hot paprika
- 1/2 teaspoon onion powder
- Sea salt and ground black pepper, to taste
- 1/4 cup agave nectar
- 2 tablespoons soy sauce
- 1/2 pound green beans

Directions:

1. In a mixing bowl, thoroughly combine all the ingredients.

2. Select the "Air Fry" function and adjust the temperature to 395 degrees F. Press the "Start" key.

3. Arrange the tofu on the air fryer oven perforated pan, making sure not to crowd them.

4. Air fry the tofu cubes for 20 minutes or until golden brown; make sure to toss them occasionally to ensure even cooking.

5. Add in the green beans and continue to cook for 5 minutes or until cooked through.

6. Bon appétit!

Nutrition:

- Info237 Calories,8.5g Fat,31.4g Carbs,13.8g Protei.

Breaded Avocado Wedges

Servings: 4
Cooking Time: 10 Minutes
Ingredients:

- 1/2 cup all-purpose flour
- 4 tablespoons vegan mayonnaise
- 1/4 cup cream of celery soup
- 2 garlic cloves, minced
- 1 cup breadcrumbs
- 1 teaspoon hot paprika
- Kosher salt and freshly ground black pepper, to taste
- 2 medium avocados, pitted, peeled and cut into wedges
- 2 teaspoon peanut oil (or toasted sesame oil)

Directions:

1. In a shallow bowl, mix the flour, mayonnaise, soup, and garlic. In another bowl, thoroughly combine breadcrumbs, hot paprika, salt, and black pepper.

2. Dip the avocado into the flour mixture. Then, dredge the avocado wedges in the breadcrumb mixture. Brush the avocado wedges with peanut oil on all sides.

3. When the display indicates "Add Food", place the avocado wedges in the air fryer oven perforated pan. Air fry them at 400 degrees F for 6 minutes.

4. Enjoy!

Nutrition:

- Info325 Calories,22.7g Fat,27.4g Carbs,5.8g Protei.

Smoked Tempeh Sandwich

Servings: 3
Cooking Time: 25 Minutes
Ingredients:

- 9 ounces tempeh, sliced
- 1 tablespoon Dijon mustard
- 2 tablespoons soy sauce
- 2 tablespoons red wine vinegar
- 2 tablespoons tomato paste
- 1 garlic clove, pressed
- 2 scallion stalks, chopped
- 1 teaspoon smoked paprika
- 6 slices whole-grain bread

Directions:

1. In a ceramic bowl, thoroughly combine all the ingredients, except for the bread. Cover and let it marinate for about 1 hour.

2. Select the "Air Fry" function and adjust the temperature to 395 degrees F. Press the "Start" key.

3. Arrange the tempeh slice on the air fryer oven perforated pan, making sure not to crowd them. Reserve the marinade.

4. Air fry the tempeh slices for 10 minutes. Flip the tempeh slices and baste them with the reserved marinade; continue to cook for 10 minutes longer or until golden brown.

5. Assemble your sandwiches with bread slices and roasted tempeh; serve immediately and enjoy!

Nutrition:

- Info451 Calories,15.2g Fat,53.2g Carbs,30.5g Protei.

Street-style Corn On The Cob

Servings: 2
Cooking Time: 15 Minutes
Ingredients:

- 2 ears corn, shucked
- 1 tablespoon olive oil
- 2 tablespoons mayonnaise
- 1 tablespoon fresh lime juice
- 1/2 teaspoon ancho chile powder
- 1 teaspoon garlic powder
- Coarse sea salt and cayenne pepper, to taste

Directions:

1. Select the "Air Fry" function and adjust the temperature to 375 degrees F. Press the "Start" key.
2. Toss your corn with olive oil.
3. Air fry your corn for 8 minutes, flipping halfway, or until the kernels are tender when pierced with a knife.
4. Toss your corn with the remaining ingredients and serve immediately.

Nutrition:

- Info244 Calories,13.7g Fat,31.1g Carbs,4.4g Protei.

Rosemary Roasted Potatoes

Servings: 4
Cooking Time: 40 Minutes
Ingredients:

- 1 ½ pounds potatoes, peeled and cut into quarters
- 2 tablespoons olive oil
- Coarse sea salt and freshly ground black pepper, to taste
- 1 teaspoon cayenne pepper
- 1 tablespoon dried rosemary, minced

Directions:

1. Select the "Air Fry" function and adjust the temperature to 400 degrees F. Press the "Start" key.
2. Toss the potato chunks with the remaining ingredients.
3. When the display indicates "Add Food", place the potato chunks in the air fryer oven perforated pan.
4. Air fry the potatoes for 35 minutes, turning them over at the halfway point.
5. Bon appétit!

Nutrition:

- Info193 Calories,7.1g Fat,30.1g Carbs,3.5g Protei.

Buffalo-style Vegan Chicken

Servings: 4
Cooking Time: 25 Minutes
Ingredients:

- 9 ounces tempeh, cut into slices
- 1/2 cup buffalo sauce
- Sea salt and ground black pepper, to season
- 1 cup breadcrumbs

Directions:

1. Toss the tempeh with the buffalo sauce, salt, and black pepper. Dredge the tempeh into the breadcrumbs.
2. Select the "Air Fry" function and adjust the temperature to 395 degrees F. Press the "Start" key.
3. Arrange the tempeh slice on the air fryer oven perforated pan, making sure not to crowd them.
4. Air fry the tempeh slices for 10 minutes. Flip the tempeh slices and continue to cook for 10 minutes longer or until golden brown.
5. Bon appétit!

Nutrition:

- Info177 Calories,7.4g Fat,14.4g Carbs,13.5g Protei.

Decadent Bourbon Carrots

Servings: 4
Cooking Time: 25 Minutes
Ingredients:

- 1 pound carrots, trimmed and cut into sticks
- 2 tablespoons olive oil
- 2 garlic cloves, minced
- 2 tablespoons balsamic vinegar
- 2 tablespoons bourbon
- 1 teaspoon stone-ground mustard
- 1/2 teaspoon cumin seeds
- Sea salt and cayenne pepper, to taste

Directions:

1. Toss all the ingredients in a mixing bowl.
2. Select the "Air Fry" function and adjust the temperature to 380 degrees F. Press the "Start" key.
3. Arrange your carrots on the parchment-lined air fryer oven perforated pan.
4. Air fry your carrots for 20 minutes or until tender and cooked through.
5. Bon appétit!

Nutrition:

- Info131 Calories,7.3g Fat,14g Carbs,1.5g Protei.

Quinoa Tofu Burgers

Servings: 4
Cooking Time: 20 Minutes
Ingredients:

- 2 cups quinoa, cooked and rinsed
- 1 teaspoon baking powder
- 4 ounces tofu, crumbled
- Kosher salt and ground black pepper, to taste
- 1/2 teaspoon cayenne pepper
- 1/2 teaspoon red pepper flakes, crushed
- 1 medium onion, chopped
- 2 cloves garlic, minced
- 1 cup breadcrumbs
- 2 tablespoons olive oil

Directions:

1. Select the "Air Fry" function and adjust the temperature to 400 degrees F. Press the "Start" key.
2. Place a sheet of parchment paper in the air fryer oven pan. Thoroughly combine all the ingredients.
3. Form the mixture into equal patties and place them in a single layer in the air fryer oven perforated pan.
4. Air fry the patties for 15 minutes or until golden brown. Serve hot and enjoy!

Nutrition:

- Info244 Calories,10.3g Fat,30.4g Carbs,8.1g Protei.

Cashew Oatmeal Muffins

Servings: 8
Cooking Time: 20 Minutes
Ingredients:

- 2 cups old-fashioned rolled oats
- 1 teaspoon baking powder
- 1/2 teaspoon baking soda
- 2 cups oat milk (or cashew milk)
- 1/2 cup cashew butter
- 2 bananas, mashed
- 1/4 cup agave syrup
- 1 teaspoon pure vanilla extract
- A pinch of kosher salt and grated nutmeg
- 1 teaspoon ground cinnamon

Directions:

1. Select the "Air Fry" function and adjust the temperature to 390 degrees F. Press the "Start" key.
2. Thoroughly combine all the ingredients. Spoon the mixture into lightly greased muffin cups.
3. Air fry the oatmeal cups for 15 minutes or until golden brown.
4. Bon appétit!

Nutrition:

- Info229 Calories,15.2g Fat,27g Carbs,6.1g Protei.

Roasted Peppers With Tofu

Servings: 4
Cooking Time: 20 Minutes
Ingredients:

- 4 bell peppers, seeded and quartered
- 1 tablespoon olive oil
- 1 tablespoon taco seasoning mix
- Sea salt and ground black pepper, to taste
- 2 garlic cloves, minced
- 2 ounces tofu, crumbled

Directions:

1. Toss all the ingredients in a mixing bowl.
2. Select the "Air Fry" function and adjust the temperature to 400 degrees F. Press the "Start" key.
3. Toss the peppers with olive oil, spices, and garlic; place them on the air fryer oven perforated pan, making sure not to crowd them.
4. Air fry the peppers and tofu for 10 minutes or until they're browned, shaking the pan once or twice during cooking.
5. Top the peppers with tofu and select the "Broil" function; continue to cook for 5 minutes more or until cooked through.
6. Bon appétit!

Nutrition:

- Info109 Calories,4.5g Fat,14.8g Carbs,3.5g Protei.

Fried Green Beans

Servings: 4
Cooking Time: 15 Minutes
Ingredients:

- 1 pound green beans
- 2 teaspoons sesame oil
- 1 tablespoon scallions, chopped
- 1 teaspoon garlic powder
- Sea salt and cayenne pepper, to taste
- 2 tablespoons nutritional yeast

Directions:

1. Toss the green beans with the other ingredients.
2. Select the "Air Fry" function and adjust the temperature to 400 degrees F. Press the "Start" key.
3. Arrange the green beans on the parchment-lined air fryer oven perforated pan.
4. Air fry the green beans for 10 minutes or until they achieve a light brown color.
5. Bon appétit!

Nutrition:

- Info79 Calories,2.5g Fat,11.5g Carbs,4.6g Protei.

Spicy Creamed Beet Salad

Servings: 4
Cooking Time: 25 Minutes
Ingredients:

- 1 pound red beets, scrubbed and diced
- 1 tablespoon olive oil
- Kosher salt and ground black pepper, to season
- 1/2 cup vegan mayonnaise
- 1 tablespoon yellow mustard
- 1/2 teaspoon ground bay leaf
- 1 red bell pepper, seeded and sliced
- 1 small chili pepper, seeded and chopped

Directions:

1. Toss the golden beets with 1 tablespoon of olive oil in a mixing bowl.
2. Select the "Air Fry" function and adjust the temperature to 400 degrees F. Press the "Start" key.
3. Arrange the beets on the air fryer oven perforated pan, making sure not to crowd them.
4. Air fry the beets for 20 minutes or until they're browned, shaking the pan once or twice during cooking.
5. Toss the roasted beets with the remaining ingredients and serve at room temperature.
6. Bon appétit!

Nutrition:

- Info284 Calories,24.3g Fat,14.4g Carbs,3g Protei.

Mediterranean-style Oatmeal Cups

Servings: 6
Cooking Time: 20 Minutes
Ingredients:

- 2 tablespoons olive oil
- 1 tablespoon coconut oil, softened
- 1 shallot, chopped
- 1 teaspoon garlic powder
- 1 teaspoon cayenne pepper
- 1 ½ cups old-fashioned rolled oats
- 3/4 cup oat milk (or rice milk)
- 1/3 cup tofu cheese, grated
- 1/4 cup sun-dried tomatoes, chopped
- 1 ounce black olives, pitted and chopped
- Sea salt and ground black pepper, to taste

Directions:

1. Select the "Air Fry" function and adjust the temperature to 390 degrees F. Press the "Start" key.
2. Thoroughly combine all the ingredients. Spoon the mixture into a greased muffin tin.

3. Air fry the oatmeal cups for 15 minutes or until golden brown.
4. Bon appétit!

Nutrition:

- Info269 Calories,12.5g Fat,3.2g Carbs,10.5g Protei.

Roasted Garlic Cabbage

Servings: 4
Cooking Time: 20 Minutes
Ingredients:

- 1 pound green cabbage, cut into wedges
- 2 tablespoons olive oil
- Kosher salt and ground black pepper, to taste
- 2 garlic cloves, minced
- 1/2 teaspoon red pepper flakes
- 1 teaspoon celery seeds

Directions:

1. Select the "Air Fry" function and adjust the temperature to 380 degrees F. Press the "Start" key.
2. Toss your cabbage with the remaining ingredients.
3. Air fry your cabbage for 15 minutes or until golden brown. Serve hot and enjoy!

Nutrition:

- Info104 Calories,7.1g Fat,10.1g Carbs,2.1g Protei.

Roasted Parmesan Fennel

Servings: 4
Cooking Time: 20 Minutes
Ingredients:

- 1 pound fennel bulb, cut into wedges
- 2 tablespoons extra-virgin olive oil
- 2 cloves garlic minced
- Sea salt and ground black pepper, to taste
- Vegan parmesan:
- 1/4 cup sesame seeds, toasted
- 1/2 teaspoon sea salt
- 2 tablespoons nutritional yeast
- 1/2 teaspoon garlic powder
- 1/2 teaspoon onion powder

Directions:

1. Toss the fennel with olive oil, garlic, salt, and black pepper.
2. Select the "Air Fry" function and adjust the temperature to 370 degrees F. Press the "Start" key.
3. Arrange the fennel wedges on the parchment-lined air fryer oven perforated pan. Air fry the fennel wedges for 15 minutes or until tender and cooked through.
4. Meanwhile, mix all the ingredients for the vegan parmesan. Toss the warm fennel with the vegan parmesan and serve immediately.
5. Enjoy!

Nutrition:

- Info179 Calories,12.8g Fat,13.5g Carbs,5.8g Protei.

Yellow Squash Gallates

Servings: 4
Cooking Time: 15 Minutes
Ingredients:
- 1 pound yellow squash
- 1 sweet onion, chopped
- 1 teaspoon garlic powder
- Kosher salt and ground black pepper, to taste
- 1 teaspoon smoked paprika
- 1 tablespoon fresh parsley leaves, chopped
- 2 tablespoons fresh cilantro leaves, chopped
- 1 cup rolled oats
- 2 tablespoons olive oil

Directions:
1. Select the "Air Fry" function and adjust the temperature to 360 degrees F. Press the "Start" key.
2. Line a baking pan with parchment paper and set it aside.
3. In a mixing bowl, thoroughly combine all the ingredients. Shape the mixture into equal patties and arrange them on the prepared baking pan.
4. When the display indicates "Add Food", cook your galettes for about 10 minutes, flipping them halfway through cooking time.
5. Bon appétit!

Nutrition:
- Info293 Calories,9.7g Fat,45.4g Carbs,8.5g Protei.

Autumn Pumpkin Pancakes

Servings: 4
Cooking Time: 15 Minutes
Ingredients:
- 1/3 cup pumpkin purée
- 1 cup coconut flour
- 1 teaspoon ground flax seeds
- 2 teaspoons brown sugar
- 1 teaspoon baking powder
- A pinch of kosher salt
- 1/2 cup coconut milk
- 2 teaspoons soy butter
- 1 teaspoon pumpkin pie spice mix

Directions:
1. In a mixing bowl, thoroughly combine the dry ingredients. In another bowl, whisk the wet ingredients. Add the wet mixture to the dry ingredients; mix to combine well.
2. Grease a baking pan with nonstick cooking oil and set it aside.
3. Select the "Air Fry" function and adjust the temperature to 350 degrees F. Press the "Start" key.
4. Cook your pancakes for about 13 minutes, working in batches, if needed. Enjoy!

Nutrition:
- Info121 Calories,9.8g Fat,7.1g Carbs,1.9g Protei.

Fried Broccoli Florets

Servings: 4
Cooking Time: 10 Minutes
Ingredients:
- 1 pound broccoli florets
- 2 teaspoons olive oil
- 2 teaspoons tahini
- 1 tablespoon nutritional yeast
- 1/2 teaspoon garlic powder
- 1/2 teaspoon onion powder
- Kosher salt and cayenne pepper, to taste

Directions:
1. Toss all the ingredients in a mixing bowl.
2. Select the "Air Fry" function and adjust the temperature to 400 degrees F. Press the "Start" key.
3. Arrange the broccoli florets on the air fryer oven perforated pan, making sure not to crowd them.
4. Air fry the broccoli florets for 6 minutes or until cooked through, tossing them once or twice during cooking time.
5. Bon appétit!

Nutrition:
- Info88 Calories,4.1g Fat,10.6g Carbs,5.1g Protei.

Easy Fried Tempeh

Servings: 4
Cooking Time: 25 Minutes
Ingredients:
- 12 ounces tempeh, sliced
- 1 tablespoon stone-ground mustard
- 2 tablespoons rice vinegar
- 1 teaspoon red pepper flakes
- 2 tablespoons soy sauce
- A few dashes of liquid smoke

Directions:
1. In a ceramic bowl, thoroughly combine all the ingredients. Cover and let it marinate for about 1 hour.
2. Select the "Air Fry" function and adjust the temperature to 395 degrees F. Press the "Start" key.
3. Arrange the tempeh slice on the air fryer oven perforated pan, making sure not to crowd them. Reserve the marinade.
4. Air fry the tempeh slices for 10 minutes. Flip the tempeh slices and baste them with the reserved marinade; continue to cook for 10 minutes longer or until golden brown.
5. Bon appétit!

Nutrition:
- Info197 Calories,11.2g Fat,10.5g Carbs,16.7g Protei.

Poultry Recipes

Juicy Duck Breast

Servings: 5
Cooking Time: 15 Minutes
Ingredients:

- 1 teaspoon olive oil
- 2 pounds duck breast
- 2 cloves garlic, chopped
- Coarse sea salt and ground black pepper, to taste
- 1 tablespoon butter
- 1 sprig fresh rosemary, chopped
- 2 sprigs fresh thyme, chopped

Directions:

1. Select the "Air Fry" function and adjust the temperature to 400 degrees F. Press the "Start" key.
2. Lightly grease the air fryer oven perforated pan with olive oil. Place aluminum foil onto the drip pan.
3. Toss duck breast with the remaining ingredients.
4. When the display indicates "Add Food", place the duck breast on the air fryer oven pan.
5. Air fry the duck breasts for about 8 minutes; flip it over and cook for 5 minutes longer or until cooked through.
6. Bon appétit!

Nutrition:

- Info419 Calories,30.6g Fat,1.3g Carbs,31.8g Protei.

Juicy Turkey Breasts

Servings: 5
Cooking Time: 45 Minutes
Ingredients:

- 2 pounds turkey breasts, boneless and skinless
- 1 cup buttermilk
- 2 garlic cloves, minced
- 2 tablespoons olive oil
- 1 tablespoon Dijon mustard
- 1 sprig fresh rosemary, chopped
- 1 sprig fresh thyme, chopped
- Kosher salt and freshly ground black pepper, to taste

Directions:

1. Place all the ingredients in a ceramic dish; let it marinate for about 1 hour.
2. Select the "Roast" function and adjust the temperature to 370 degrees F. Press the "Start" key.

3. Place the turkey in the air fryer oven perforated pan. Place aluminum foil onto the drip pan.
4. Roast the turkey for about 20 minutes; flip it over and cook for 15 minutes longer or until the turkey reaches an internal temperature of 170 degrees F on a meat thermometer.
5. Let the turkey rest for 10 minutes before slicing and serving. Enjoy!

Nutrition:

- Info386 Calories,18.6g Fat,2.8g Carbs,42.2g Protei.

Asian-style Glazed Duck Breast

Servings: 4
Cooking Time: 15 Minutes
Ingredients:

- 1 ½ pounds duck breasts, skin-on
- 1/4 cup honey
- 2 tablespoons soy sauce
- 2 tablespoons rice wine
- 1 teaspoon ginger, peeled and grated
- 2 tablespoons sesame oil
- Sea salt and ground black pepper, to taste
- 1 teaspoon cayenne pepper

Directions:

1. Select the "Air Fry" function and adjust the temperature to 400 degrees F. Press the "Start" key.
2. Lightly grease the air fryer oven perforated pan with olive oil. Place aluminum foil onto the drip pan.
3. Toss the duck breast with the remaining ingredients.
4. When the display indicates "Add Food", place the duck breast on the air fryer oven pan.
5. Air fry the duck breasts for about 8 minutes; flip it over and cook for 5 minutes longer or until cooked through.
6. Bon appétit!

Nutrition:

- Info378 Calories,18.3g Fat,21.2g Carbs,31.6g Protei.

Classic Chicken Cutlets

Servings: 4
Cooking Time: 25 Minutes
Ingredients:

- 1 ½ pounds chicken breasts, sliced
- 1 tablespoon butter, melted
- 2 eggs, whisked
- 1/2 teaspoon cayenne pepper
- Kosher salt and ground black pepper, to taste
- 1 cup seasoned breadcrumbs

Directions:

1. Select the "Air Fry" function and adjust the temperature to 360 degrees F. Press the "Start" key.
2. Toss the chicken with the remaining ingredients.
3. When the display indicates "Add Food", place the chicken tenders in the parchment-lined air fryer oven pan.
4. Air Fry the chicken for about 10 minutes; flip it over and cook for 10 minutes longer or until the chicken reaches an internal temperature of 160 degrees F on a meat thermometer.
5. Bon appétit!

Nutrition:

- Info465 Calories,20.7g Fat,21.1g Carbs,40.7g Protei.

Restaurant-style Chicken Tenders

Servings: 4
Cooking Time: 20 Minutes
Ingredients:

- 1 tablespoon olive oil
- 1 large egg
- 1 tablespoon butter, melted
- 1 tablespoon fresh parsley leaves, chopped
- 2 garlic cloves, minced
- Sea salt and ground black pepper, to taste
- 1 ½ pounds chicken tenders
- 1 cup breadcrumbs
- 1/4 cup Pecorino cheese, grated

Directions:

1. Select the "Air Fry" function and adjust the temperature to 350 degrees F. Press the "Start" key. Lightly grease the air fryer oven perforated pan with olive oil.
2. In a shallow bowl, whisk the egg, butter, parsley, garlic, salt, and black pepper. Add the chicken tenders to the bowl and toss until well coated on all sides.

3. In another shallow bowl, mix the breadcrumbs and cheese. Roll the chicken tenders over the breadcrumb mixture until well coated on all sides.
4. When the display indicates "Add Food", place the tenders in the air fryer oven perforated pan. Air fry them for 15 minutes.
5. Bon appétit!

Nutrition:

- Info422 Calories,25.6g Fat,5.3g Carbs,39.4g Protei.

Herb Lemony Chicken Breast

Servings: 5
Cooking Time: 50 Minutes
Ingredients:

- 2 pounds bone-in and skin-on chicken breast
- 4 tablespoons olive oil
- 2 tablespoons fresh lemon juice
- 2 garlic cloves, minced
- 1/2 cup white wine
- 1/2 teaspoon cumin seeds
- 2 sprigs fresh rosemary
- 2 sprigs fresh thyme
- 1 teaspoon smoked paprika
- Sea salt and ground black pepper, to taste

Directions:

1. Select the "Roast" function and adjust the temperature to 360 degrees F. Press the "Start" key.
2. Place the chicken along with the other ingredients in the air fryer oven perforated pan. Place aluminum foil onto the drip pan.
3. Roast the chicken for about 20 minutes; flip it over and cook for 20 minutes longer or until the chicken reaches an internal temperature of 160 degrees F on a meat thermometer.
4. Transfer the chicken breast to a cutting board and let it rest for 10 minutes before slicing and serving.
5. Bon appétit!

Nutrition:

- Info416 Calories,27.7g Fat,1.5g Carbs,38.1g Protei.

Favorite Turkey Meatballs

Servings: 4
Cooking Time: 20 Minutes
Ingredients:
- 1 tablespoon olive oil
- 1 pound ground turkey
- 1/2 cup Pecorino cheese, grated
- 1/4 cup breadcrumbs
- 2 tablespoons parsley, chopped
- 2 tablespoons basil, chopped
- 2 tablespoons chives, chopped
- Kosher salt and ground black pepper, to taste
- 1 teaspoon garlic, minced
- 1 teaspoon cayenne pepper
- 1 medium egg

Directions:
1. Select the "Air Fry" function and adjust the temperature to 350 degrees F. Press the "Start" key.
2. Place a sheet of parchment paper in the air fryer oven pan.
3. In a mixing bowl, thoroughly combine the remaining ingredients. Then, drop rounds of the mixture in a single layer onto the prepared pan using a small scoop.
4. Air fry the meatballs for 10 minutes; turn the meatballs over and increase the temperature to 400 degrees F. Air fry for a further 5 minutes to brown the outsides of the meatballs, until they reach an internal temperature of 165 degrees F.
5. Bon appétit!

Nutrition:
- Info291 Calories,18.6g Fat,3.3g Carbs,28.4g Protei.

Festive Chicken Rolls

Servings: 4
Cooking Time: 25 Minutes
Ingredients:
- 1 pound chicken fillets
- Sea salt and cayenne pepper, to season
- 4 ounces cooked ham, diced
- 4 ounces Colby cheese, diced
- 2 tablespoons butter, melted
- 1 teaspoon Dijon mustard
- 1/2 cup cornflakes cereal, crushed

Directions:
1. Select the "Air Fry" function and adjust the temperature to 360 degrees F. Press the "Start" key.
2. Place a sheet of parchment paper in the air fryer oven pan.
3. Pat the chicken dry and season them with salt and cayenne pepper.
4. In a mixing bowl, thoroughly combine the ham, cheese, butter, and mustard. Divide the stuffing between the chicken fillets and roll them up. Roll them over the crushed cornflakes.
5. Arrange the chicken rolls in the air fryer oven perforated pan.
6. Air fry the chicken rolls for about 10 minutes; turn them over and continue to cook for 10 minutes longer or until the chicken reaches an internal temperature of 160 degrees F on a meat thermometer.
7. Bon appétit!

Nutrition:
- Info461 Calories,33.1g Fat,6.3g Carbs,33.6g Protei.

Kid-friendly Chicken Nuggets

Servings: 5
Cooking Time: 20 Minutes
Ingredients:
- 1 teaspoon olive oil
- 2 pounds boneless, skinless chicken breasts, cut into 1-inch-thick strips
- 1 egg, beaten
- 1 cup all-purpose flour
- Coarse sea salt and ground black pepper, to taste
- 1 cup tortilla chips, crushed

Directions:
1. Select the "Air Fry" function and adjust the temperature to 350 degrees F. Press the "Start" key. Then, grease the air fryer oven perforated pan with olive oil.
2. Pat the chicken dry and set it aside.
3. In a shallow bowl, whisk the egg until pale and frothy; gradually add in the flour, salt, and black pepper. Add the chicken tenders to the bowl and toss until well coated on all sides.
4. In another shallow bowl, place the crushed tortilla chips. Roll the chicken strips over the crushed tortilla chips until well coated on all sides.
5. When the display indicates "Add Food", place the tenders in the air fryer oven perforated pan. Air fry them for 15 minutes.
6. Serve warm and enjoy!

Nutrition:
- Info440 Calories,13.2g Fat,37.5g Carbs,42.4g Protei.

Grandma's Chicken Roulade

Servings: 4
Cooking Time: 25 Minutes
Ingredients:

- 1 pound chicken fillets
- Sea salt and ground black pepper, to taste
- 1 cup goat cheese, crumbled
- 1 teaspoon fresh thyme leaves, chopped
- 1 teaspoon fresh rosemary leaves, chopped
- 4 ounces smoked bacon, diced
- 1 bell pepper, seeded and diced

Directions:

1. Select the "Air Fry" function and adjust the temperature to 360 degrees F. Press the "Start" key.
2. Place a sheet of parchment paper in the air fryer oven pan.
3. Pat the chicken dry and season them with salt and black pepper.
4. In a mixing bowl, thoroughly combine the remaining ingredients. Divide the stuffing between the chicken fillets and roll them up.
5. Arrange the chicken rolls in the air fryer oven perforated pan.
6. Air fry the chicken rolls for about 10 minutes; flip it over and cook for 10 minutes longer or until the chicken reaches an internal temperature of 160 degrees F on a meat thermometer.
7. Bon appétit!

Nutrition:

- Info492 Calories,38.2g Fat,2.7g Carbs,33.2g Protei.

Roast Duck Breast

Servings: 5
Cooking Time: 15 Minutes
Ingredients:

- 1 teaspoon olive oil
- 2 pounds duck breast
- Coarse sea salt and ground black pepper, to taste
- 1 tablespoon butter
- 1 teaspoon garlic, pressed
- 1 teaspoon hot paprika
- 1 teaspoon dried parsley flakes

Directions:

1. Select the "Air Fry" function and adjust the temperature to 400 degrees F. Press the "Start" key.
2. Lightly grease the air fryer oven perforated pan with olive oil. Place aluminum foil onto the drip pan.
3. Toss the duck breast with the remaining ingredients.

4. When the display indicates "Add Food", place the duck breast on the air fryer oven pan.
5. Air fry the duck breasts for about 8 minutes; flip it over and cook for 5 minutes longer or until cooked through.
6. Bon appétit!

Nutrition:

- Info372 Calories,28.2g Fat,3.9g Carbs,23.5g Protei.

Garlicky Butter Turkey

Servings: 5
Cooking Time: 40 Minutes
Ingredients:

- 1 ½ pounds turkey breast, bone-in, skin-on
- Kosher salt and freshly ground black pepper, to taste
- 4 tablespoons butter, melted
- 4 cloves garlic, minced
- 1 teaspoon dried rosemary

Directions:

1. Select the "Roast" function and adjust the temperature to 370 degrees F. Press the "Start" key.
2. Place the turkey in the air fryer oven perforated pan. Place aluminum foil onto the drip pan.
3. Roast the turkey for about 20 minutes; flip it over and cook for 15 minutes longer or until the turkey reaches an internal temperature of 170 degrees F on a meat thermometer.
4. Let the turkey rest for 10 minutes before slicing and serving. Enjoy!

Nutrition:

- Info327 Calories,16.6g Fat,1.1g Carbs,35.7g Protei.

Butter Sage Turkey Cutlets

Servings: 5
Cooking Time: 20 Minutes
Ingredients:

- 2 pounds turkey breast cutlets
- 2 tablespoons butter, melted
- 1 teaspoon ground sage
- Sea salt and ground black pepper, to season

Directions:

1. Select the "Air Fry" function and adjust the temperature to 360 degrees F. Press the "Start" key.
2. Toss the turkey breast cutlets with the other ingredients; now, place them on the parchment-lined air fryer oven perforated pan.
3. Air fry the turkey cutlets for about 8 minutes; turn the cutlets over and cook for 7 minutes longer or until cooked through.
4. Bon appétit!

Nutrition:

- Info327 Calories,17.4g Fat,0.1g Carbs,39.7g Protei.

Classic Festive Turkey

Servings: 5
Cooking Time: 40 Minutes
Ingredients:

- 2 pounds turkey, giblet removed, rinsed and pat dry
- Kosher salt ground black pepper, to taste
- 1 teaspoon dried thyme
- 1 teaspoon ground rosemary
- Sea salt and freshly ground black pepper
- 1 teaspoon paprika
- 1 tablespoon agave syrup
- 2 tablespoon olive oil

Directions:

1. Select the "Roast" function and adjust the temperature to 360 degrees F. Set the oven to "Rotate" and set time to 35 minutes. Press the "Start" key.
2. When the display indicates "Add Food", place the turkey legs in the rotisserie basket.
3. Roast the turkey until it reaches an internal temperature of 165 degrees F on a meat thermometer.
4. Bon appétit!

Nutrition:

- Info440 Calories,34.3g Fat,4.5g Carbs,24.3g Protei.

Thanksgiving Turkey Legs

Servings: 5
Cooking Time: 40 Minutes
Ingredients:

- 2 pounds turkey legs
- Sea salt and ground black pepper, to taste
- 2 tablespoons butter
- 1 teaspoon dried parsley flakes
- 1 teaspoon dried rosemary
- 1 teaspoon dried oregano
- 1 teaspoon dried basil

Directions:

1. Select the "Roast" function and adjust the temperature to 355 degrees F. Set the oven to "Rotate" and set the time to 35 minutes. Press the "Start" key.
2. When the display indicates "Add Food", place the turkey legs in the rotisserie basket.
3. Roast the turkey until it reaches an internal temperature of 165 degrees F on a meat thermometer.
4. Bon appétit!

Nutrition:

- Info327 Calories,16.6g Fat,1.1g Carbs,35.7g Protei.

Spicy Chicken Frittata

Servings: 4
Cooking Time: 20 Minutes
Ingredients:

- 1 large tomato, chopped
- 1 jalapeño pepper, seeded and minced
- 1 bell pepper, seeded and chopped
- 1 small onion, chopped
- Sea salt and ground black pepper, to taste
- 2 tablespoons olive oil
- 1 clove garlic, pressed
- 8 eggs
- 4 tablespoons cream cheese
- 1 pound ground chicken

Directions:

1. Select the "Air Fry" function and adjust the temperature to 330 degrees F. Press the "Start" key.
2. Grease a baking pan with cooking oil and set it aside.
3. In a mixing bowl, thoroughly combine all the ingredients. Pour the mixture into the prepared baking pan.
4. Bake your frittata for 15 minutes or until a toothpick comes out dry and clean.
5. Bon appétit!

Nutrition:

- Info422 Calories,28.4g Fat,8.1g Carbs,33.1g Protei.

Ranch Chicken Wings

Servings: 5
Cooking Time: 25 Minutes
Ingredients:

- 2 pounds chicken wings
- 6 tablespoons mayonnaise
- 2 tablespoons dry ranch dressing
- Sea salt and ground black pepper, to taste

Directions:

1. Select the "Air Fry" function and adjust the temperature to 375 degrees F. Press the "Start" key.
2. Place a sheet of parchment paper in the air fryer oven pan. Toss the chicken wings with the remaining ingredients.
3. Arrange the chicken wings in a single layer in the air fryer oven perforated pan.
4. Air fry the chicken wings for 10 minutes; turn them over and air fry for a further 10 minutes or until they are crunchy and cooked through.
5. Bon appétit!

Nutrition:

- Info372 Calories,21.5g Fat,1.3g Carbs,40.2g Protei.

Turkey And Mushroom Croquettes

Servings: 5
Cooking Time: 20 Minutes
Ingredients:

- 1 pound ground chicken
- 4 ounces brown mushrooms, chopped
- ¼ cup whole milk
- 2 medium eggs, beaten
- 1 small onion, chopped
- 1 cup breadcrumbs
- 1 tablespoon butter
- 1 tablespoon olive oil

Directions:

1. Select the "Air Fry" function and adjust the temperature to 350 degrees F. Press the "Start" key.
2. Place a sheet of parchment paper in the air fryer oven pan.
3. In a mixing bowl, thoroughly combine all the ingredients. Then, drop rounds of the mixture in a single layer onto the prepared pan using a small scoop.
4. Air fry the croquettes for 10 minutes; turn the croquettes over and increase the temperature to 400 degrees F. Air fry for a further 5 minutes to brown the outsides of the croquettes.
5. Bon appétit!

Nutrition:

- Info288 Calories,15.8g Fat,13.3g Carbs,21.1g Protei.

Kid-friendly Chicken Croquettes

Servings: 4
Cooking Time: 20 Minutes
Ingredients:

- 2 tablespoons unsalted butter
- 1 pound ground chicken
- 2 ounces, bacon
- Sea salt and freshly ground pepper, to taste
- 1 cup breadcrumbs
- 1/4 cup whole milk
- 2 medium eggs

Directions:

1. Select the "Air Fry" function and adjust the temperature to 350 degrees F. Press the "Start" key.
2. Place a sheet of parchment paper in the air fryer oven pan.

3. In a mixing bowl, thoroughly combine all the ingredients. Then, drop rounds of the mixture in a single layer onto the prepared pan using a small scoop.
4. Air fry the croquettes for 10 minutes; turn the croquettes over and increase the temperature to 400 degrees F. Air fry for a further 5 minutes to brown the outsides of the croquettes.
5. Bon appétit!

Nutrition:

- Info397 Calories,28.1g Fat,8.5g Carbs,27.1g Protei.

Herbed Chicken Drumsticks

Servings: 4
Cooking Time: 30 Minutes
Ingredients:

- 1 ½ pounds chicken drumsticks
- 2 teaspoons olive
- 1 teaspoon paprika
- Kosher salt and ground black pepper, to taste
- 1 teaspoon garlic powder
- 2 sprigs rosemary, chopped
- 1 sprig thyme, chopped

Directions:

1. Select the "Air Fry" function and adjust the temperature to 400 degrees F. Press the "Start" key.
2. Lightly grease the air fryer oven perforated pan with olive oil.
3. Poke about 10 holes in the skin of each drumstick. Toss the chicken drumsticks with the remaining ingredients.
4. When the display indicates "Add Food", place the drumsticks in the air fryer oven perforated pan.
5. Roast the chicken drumsticks for about 25 minutes, flipping them halfway through cooking.
6. Bon appétit!

Nutrition:

- Info378 Calories,21.8g Fat,2.3g Carbs,44.1g Protei.

Creamed Chicken Salad

Servings: 4
Cooking Time: 20 Minutes
Ingredients:

- 1 ½ pounds boneless, skinless chicken breasts, cut into bite-sized chunks
- 1 teaspoon olive oil
- Salad:
- 2 stalks celery, chopped
- 1 bell pepper, seeded and chopped
- 1/2 cup Kalamata olives, pitted and sliced
- 1 small onion, chopped
- 1 small head Romaine lettuce, torn into pieces
- Dressing:
- 6 tablespoons mayonnaise
- 2 tablespoons sour cream
- 1 teaspoon white vinegar
- 1 teaspoon Dijon mustard
- Sea salt and ground black pepper, to taste

Directions:

1. Select the "Roast" function and adjust the temperature to 380 degrees F. Press the "Start" key.
2. Toss the chicken chunks with olive oil until well coated on all sides. Place the chicken in a baking pan.
3. When the display indicates "Add Food", place the baking pan on the cooking tray.
4. Roast the chicken in the preheated air fryer oven for 15 minutes or until cooked through.
5. Toss the chicken with the remaining salad ingredients. Mix all the dressing ingredients until well combined. Dress your salad and enjoy!

Nutrition:

- Info441 Calories,27.1g Fat,10.3g Carbs,39.6g Protei.

Mustard Chicken Breasts

Servings: 5
Cooking Time: 25 Minutes
Ingredients:

- 1 teaspoon olive oil
- 2 pounds chicken breast, skinless and boneless
- 1 tablespoon coarse-ground mustard
- 1 tablespoon honey
- Salt and ground black pepper, to taste
- 1 teaspoon red pepper flakes, crushed
- 1/2 teaspoon garlic powder

Directions:

1. Select the "Roast" function and adjust the temperature to 360 degrees F. Press the "Start" key.

2. Toss the chicken with the remaining ingredients in the air fryer oven perforated pan. Place aluminum foil onto the drip pan.
3. Roast the chicken for about 10 minutes; flip it over and cook for 10 minutes longer or until the chicken reaches an internal temperature of 160 degrees F on a meat thermometer.
4. Bon appétit!

Nutrition:

- Info344 Calories,18.2g Fat,5g Carbs,38.4g Protei.

Restaurant-style Chicken Gyros

Servings: 4
Cooking Time: 20 Minutes
Ingredients:

- 1 pound boneless and skinless chicken breast, cut into strips
- 4 tablespoons Greek yogurt
- 1 small lemon, juiced
- 1 tablespoon olive oil
- 2 cloves garlic, minced
- 1 tablespoon Dijon mustard
- 1 teaspoon dried oregano
- Sea salt and ground black pepper, to taste
- 4 pita bread
- 4 tablespoons Tzatziki sauce
- 8 lettuce leaves
- 1 medium tomato, sliced

Directions:

1. Select the "Roast" function and adjust the temperature to 380 degrees F. Press the "Start" key.
2. Toss the chicken strips with Greek yogurt, lemon juice, olive oil, garlic, mustard, oregano, salt, and black pepper.
3. Place the chicken in a baking pan. When the display indicates "Add Food", place the baking pan on the cooking tray.
4. Roast the chicken in the preheated air fryer oven for 15 minutes or until the chicken reaches an internal temperature of 165 degrees F on a meat thermometer.
5. Assemble your gyros with pita bread, Tzatziki sauce, lettuce leaves, and tomato. Enjoy!

Nutrition:

- Info417 Calories,14.8g Fat,37.9g Carbs,31.1g Protei.

Garlic Parmesan Chicken Wings

Servings: 4

Cooking Time: 25 Minutes

Ingredients:

- 1 ½ pound chicken wings
- Sea salt and ground black pepper, to season
- 1 teaspoon cayenne pepper
- 1/4 cup butter
- 2 cloves garlic, pressed
- 1/2 cup parmesan cheese, preferably freshly grated

Directions:

1. Select the "Air Fry" function and adjust the temperature to 375 degrees F. Press the "Start" key.
2. Place a sheet of parchment paper in the air fryer oven pan. Toss the chicken wings with the remaining ingredients.
3. Arrange the chicken wings in a single layer in the air fryer oven perforated pan.
4. Air fry the chicken wings for 10 minutes; turn them over and air fry for a further 10 minutes or until they are browned and crunchy.
5. Bon appétit!

Nutrition:

- Info487 Calories,37.6g Fat,3.5g Carbs,33.8g Protei.

Louisiana-style Stuffed Chicken

Servings: 4

Cooking Time: 25 Minutes

Ingredients:

- 1 ½ pound chicken fillets
- Sea salt and ground black pepper, to taste
- 1 teaspoon cayenne pepper
- 2 tablespoons Louisiana-style hot sauce
- 8 ounces smoked pork sausage, crumbled
- 6 ounces parmesan cheese, grated
- 1 cup breadcrumbs

Directions:

1. Select the "Air Fry" function and adjust the temperature to 360 degrees F. Press the "Start" key.
2. Pat the chicken dry and season them with salt, black pepper, and cayenne pepper.
3. In a mixing bowl, thoroughly combine the hot sauce, sausage, and cheese. Divide the stuffing between the chicken fillets and roll them up.
4. Roll them over the breadcrumbs and secure with toothpicks.

5. Air fry the stuffed chicken for about 10 minutes; flip it over and cook for 10 minutes longer or until the chicken reaches an internal temperature of 160 degrees F on a meat thermometer.
6. Bon appétit!

Nutrition:

- Info602 Calories,34.6g Fat,13.3g Carbs,56.1g Protei.

Herb Chicken Cutlets

Servings: 4

Cooking Time: 25 Minutes

Ingredients:

- 1 ½ pounds boneless, skinless chicken fillets
- 1 tablespoon Dijon mustard
- 4 tablespoons mayonnaise
- 1/2 cup crackers, crushed
- Kosher salt and ground black pepper, to taste
- 1 teaspoon dried rosemary
- 1 teaspoon dried thyme
- 1/2 teaspoon garlic powder
- 1 teaspoon hot paprika

Directions:

1. Select the "Air Fry" function and adjust the temperature to 360 degrees F. Press the "Start" key.
2. Toss the chicken with the remaining ingredients in the air fryer oven perforated pan. Place aluminum foil onto the drip pan.
3. Air fry the chicken for about 10 minutes; flip it over and cook for 10 minutes longer or until the chicken reaches an internal temperature of 160 degrees F on a meat thermometer.
4. Bon appétit!

Nutrition:

- Info472 Calories,36.2g Fat,2.5g Carbs,32.3g Protei.

Curried Chicken Cups

Servings: 4
Cooking Time: 20 Minutes
Ingredients:

- 1 pound chicken breast, boneless, skinless, and chopped
- 1 tablespoon butter, melted
- 2 tablespoons scallions, chopped
- 1 teaspoon curry paste
- 2 cups self-rising flour
- 2 large eggs, beaten
- Sea salt and ground black pepper, to taste

Directions:

1. Select the "Bake" function and adjust the temperature to 380 degrees F and the time to 15 minutes. Press the "Start" key.
2. Meanwhile, brush silicone muffin cups with nonstick cooking oil. Mix all the ingredients until well combined. Divide the mixture between the muffin cups.
3. When the display indicates "Add Food", place the muffin cups on the cooking tray.
4. Bake the muffins in the preheated air fryer oven until cooked through. Bon appétit!

Nutrition:

- Info485 Calories,16.4g Fat,48.1g Carbs,33.3g Protei.

Italian-style Turkey Tenderloin

Servings: 6
Cooking Time: 45 Minutes
Ingredients:

- 6 tablespoons butter, softened
- 2 cloves garlic, minced
- 1 tablespoon Italian seasoning
- Coarse sea salt and ground black pepper, to taste
- 2 pounds turkey tenderloin
- 1 teaspoon spicy brown mustard
- 1/4 cup white wine
- 1/2 cup chicken stock

Directions:

1. Select the "Roast" function and adjust the temperature to 370 degrees F. Press the "Start" key.
2. Place the turkey along with the other ingredients in a baking pan. Place aluminum foil onto the drip pan.
3. Roast the turkey for about 20 minutes; flip it over and cook for 15 minutes longer or until the turkey reaches an internal temperature of 170 degrees F on a meat thermometer.
4. Let the turkey rest for 10 minutes before slicing and serving. Enjoy!

Nutrition:

- Info421 Calories,35.6g Fat,2.2g Carbs,21.1g Protei.

Creamy Turkey Salad

Servings: 5
Cooking Time: 45 Minutes + Chilling Time
Ingredients:

- 1 pound turkey breast tenderloin
- 1/2 cup mayonnaise
- 4 tablespoons Greek-style yogurt
- 1 teaspoon yellow mustard
- 1 tablespoon white vinegar
- 1 teaspoon honey
- 1 small red onion, thinly sliced
- 1 medium cucumber, diced
- 2 bell peppers, seeded and sliced
- 1 cup baby spinach

Directions:

1. Select the "Roast" function and adjust the temperature to 370 degrees F. Press the "Start" key.
2. Place the turkey in a lightly oiled baking pan. Place aluminum foil onto the drip pan.
3. Roast the turkey for about 20 minutes; flip it over and cook for 15 minutes longer or until the turkey reaches an internal temperature of 170 degrees F on a meat thermometer.
4. Let the turkey rest for 10 minutes before slicing and serving. Cut the turkey into strips and add in the other ingredients.
5. Toss to combine well and serve well-chilled. Enjoy!

Nutrition:

- Info331 Calories,23.1g Fat,6.2g Carbs,23.4g Protei.

Ground Chicken Muffins

Servings: 6
Cooking Time: 20 Minutes
Ingredients:

- 1 ½ pounds ground chicken
- 1 tablespoon olive oil
- 2 eggs
- 1/2 cup tomato paste
- 1 cup instant oats
- 1 teaspoon paprika
- 1 teaspoon Dijon mustard
- Sea salt and ground black pepper, to taste
- 1 teaspoon chili powder
- 2 garlic cloves, minced
- 2 tablespoons scallions, chopped

Directions:

1. Select the "Bake" function and adjust the temperature to 360 degrees F and the time to 15 minutes. Press the "Start" key.
2. Meanwhile, brush silicone muffin cups with nonstick cooking oil. Mix all the ingredients until well combined. Divide the mixture between the muffin cups.
3. When the display indicates "Add Food", place the muffin cups on the cooking tray.
4. Bake the muffins in the preheated air fryer oven until cooked through. Bon appétit!

Nutrition:

- Info330 Calories,14.8g Fat,23.3g Carbs,27.3g Protei.

Fish And Seafood Recipes

Louisiana-style Shrimp Tacos

Servings: 4
Cooking Time: 15 Minutes
Ingredients:

- 1 pound jumbo shrimp, peeled and deveined
- 2 tablespoons olive oil
- 2 tablespoons taco seasoning mix
- Sea salt and freshly-cracked black pepper, to taste
- 1 tablespoon Louisiana-style hot pepper sauce
- 4 tablespoons mayonnaise
- 8 small corn tortillas
- 1 avocado, peeled, pitted and sliced
- 1 red onion, thinly sliced

Directions:

1. Select the "Air Fry" function and adjust the temperature to 400 degrees F. Press the "Start" key.
2. In a mixing bowl, toss the shrimp with olive oil and spices.
3. When the display indicates "Add Food", place the shrimp in the air fryer oven perforated pan. Air fry the shrimp for 7 to 8 minutes or until pink and opaque.
4. To serve, place tortillas on each plate and top each with shrimp and the remaining ingredients.
5. Bon appétit!

Nutrition:

- Info471 Calories,27.4g Fat,29.6g Carbs,27.4g Protei.

Greek-style Sardine Cakes

Servings: 4
Cooking Time: 15 Minutes
Ingredients:

- 1/2 pound zucchini, grated
- 12 ounces sardines, drained and chopped
- 4 tablespoons scallions, chopped
- 1 teaspoon garlic, minced
- 1 large egg, whisked
- 1 red onion, minced
- 1 celery stick, minced
- 1/2 cup breadcrumbs

Directions:

1. Select the "Air Fry" function and adjust the temperature to 390 degrees F. Press the "Start" key.
2. Place a sheet of parchment paper in the air fryer oven pan. Thoroughly combine all the ingredients.
3. Form the mixture into four patties and place them in a single layer in the air fryer oven perforated pan.
4. Air fry the patties for 12 minutes, turning them over halfway through.
5. Bon appétit!

Nutrition:

- Info275 Calories,12g Fat,15.6g Carbs,25.5g Protei.

Spicy Peppery Tiger Prawn Salad

Servings: 4
Cooking Time: 10 Minutes
Ingredients:
- 1 pound tiger prawns, peeled and deveined
- 2 garlic cloves, minced
- 2 tablespoons fresh parsley, roughly chopped
- 2 tablespoons fresh cilantro, roughly chopped
- 2 scallion stalks, chopped
- 2 bell peppers, sliced
- 1 red chili pepper, sliced
- Sea salt and ground black pepper, to taste
- 1/4 cup extra-virgin olive oil
- 1 teaspoon yellow mustard

Directions:
1. Select the "Air Fry" function and adjust the temperature to 390 degrees F. Press the "Start" key.
2. In a mixing bowl, toss the shrimp with 1 teaspoon of olive oil.
3. When the display indicates "Add Food", place your prawns in the air fryer oven perforated pan.
4. Air fry your prawns for 7 to 8 minutes or until pink and opaque. Toss your prawns with the other salad ingredients and serve well-chilled.
5. Bon appétit!

Nutrition:
- Info253 Calories,14.4g Fat,7.9g Carbs,25.5g Protei.

Authentic Mediterranean-style Shrimp

Servings: 4
Cooking Time: 10 Minutes
Ingredients:
- 1 egg, whisked
- 2 tablespoons yogurt
- 1/2 teaspoon mustard seeds
- 1/2 cup all-purpose flour
- Sea salt and ground black pepper, to taste
- 2 teaspoons olive oil
- 1 cup tortilla chips, crushed
- 1 pound raw shrimp, peeled and deveined

Directions:
1. In a shallow bowl, mix the egg, yogurt, mustard seeds, flour, salt, and black pepper. In another shallow bowl, place the olive oil and crushed tortilla chips.

2. Dredge the shrimp in the egg mixture. Then, dip the strips in crushed tortilla chips, coating them completely.
3. Select the "Air Fry" function and adjust the temperature to 390 degrees F. Press the "Start" key.
4. Arrange the shrimp on the air fryer oven perforated pan, making sure not to crowd them. Air fry the shrimp for 9 minutes or until golden brown.
5. Bon appétit!

Nutrition:
- Info255 Calories,6.2g Fat,19.5g Carbs,27.7g Protei.

Authentic Fish Burritos

Servings: 4
Cooking Time: 15 Minutes
Ingredients:
- 1 large egg
- 1 teaspoon Mexican oregano
- 1 cup seasoned breadcrumbs
- 2 teaspoons olive oil
- 1 pound cod fish fillet, cut into strips
- 8 small flour tortillas (or corn tortillas)
- 1/2 cup guacamole sauce

Directions:
1. Whisk the egg with oregano in a shallow bowl.
2. In another shallow bowl, mix the seasoned breadcrumbs and olive oil.
3. Dredge the fish strips in the egg mixture. Then, dip the strips in the breadcrumb mixture, coating them completely and shaking off any excess.
4. Select the "Air Fry" function and adjust the temperature to 400 degrees F. Press the "Start" key.
5. Arrange the fish strips on the air fryer oven perforated pan, making sure not to crowd them. Air fry the fish for 10 minutes or until it is thoroughly cooked.
6. Assemble your burritos with warm fish strips, tortillas, and guacamole sauce. Serve immediately and enjoy!

Nutrition:
- Info339 Calories,7.8g Fat,38.4g Carbs,25.3g Protei.

Classic Fried Sea Scallops

Servings: 4
Cooking Time: 15 Minutes
Ingredients:

- 1 pound sea scallops
- 1 teaspoon garlic, minced
- 1 teaspoon onion powder
- 2 teaspoons olive oil
- Kosher salt and ground black pepper, to taste
- 1 teaspoon paprika
- 1 teaspoon dried basil
- 1 teaspoon dried oregano

Directions:

1. Select the "Air Fry" function and adjust the temperature to 400 degrees F. Press the "Start" key.
2. In a mixing bowl, toss the sea scallops with the other ingredients.
3. When the display indicates "Add Food", place the sea scallops in the air fryer oven perforated pan.
4. Air fry the sea scallops for 10 minutes or until pink and opaque.
5. Bon appétit!

Nutrition:

- Info346 Calories,6.8g Fat,4.6g Carbs,37.1g Protei.

Sea Scallop Salad

Servings: 4
Cooking Time: 15 Minutes
Ingredients:

- 1 pound sea scallops
- Kosher salt and ground black pepper, to taste
- 1 teaspoon cayenne pepper
- 1/4 cup extra-virgin olive oil
- 2 tablespoons fresh chives, chopped
- 2 tablespoons fresh mint, chopped
- 2 tablespoons fresh parsley, chopped
- 2 tablespoons balsamic vinegar
- 1 red onion, chopped
- 2 garlic cloves, minced
- 2 teaspoons honey
- 1 teaspoon Dijon mustard
- 2 cups mix salad greens
- 1 carrot, julienned
- 1 bell pepper, sliced
- 1 cup grape tomatoes, halved

Directions:

1. Select the "Air Fry" function and adjust the temperature to 400 degrees F. Press the "Start" key.
2. When the display indicates "Add Food", place the sea scallops in the air fryer oven perforated pan.
3. Air fry the sea scallops for 10 minutes or until pink and opaque. Add in the remaining ingredients and toss to combine. Bon appétit!

Nutrition:

- Info259 Calories,14g Fat,17.3g Carbs,15.5g Protei.

Restaurant-style Fish Fingers

Servings: 5
Cooking Time: 15 Minutes
Ingredients:

- 1 ½ pounds cod fillets, cut into bite-sized strips
- 2 tablespoons olive oil
- 1 egg, beaten
- 1/4 cup milk
- 1 teaspoon garlic salt
- Freshly ground black pepper, to season
- 1/2 cup dry pancake mix
- 1/2 cup seasoned breadcrumbs

Directions:

1. In a shallow bowl, mix the olive oil, egg, milk, garlic salt, black pepper, dry pancake mix.
2. In another shallow bowl, mix the remaining ingredients.
3. Dredge the fish strips in the oil/egg mixture. Then, dip the strips in the breadcrumb mixture, coating them completely and shaking off any excess.
4. Select the "Air Fry" function and adjust the temperature to 400 degrees F. Press the "Start" key.
5. Arrange the fish strips on the air fryer oven perforated pan, making sure not to crowd them. Air fry the fish for 10 minutes or until it is thoroughly cooked.
6. Bon appétit!

Nutrition:

- Info255 Calories,7.4g Fat,18.6g Carbs,24.7g Protei.

Crispy Codfish Fillets

Servings: 4

Cooking Time: 15 Minutes

Ingredients:

- 1 pound codfish fillets
- 1 tablespoon olive oil
- 1 teaspoon Old Bay seasoning mix
- Kosher salt and ground black pepper, to taste
- 1/2 cup very fine cornmeal
- 1/4 cup all-purpose flour
- 1 teaspoon hot paprika

Directions:

1. Select the "Air Fry" function and adjust the temperature to 400 degrees F. Set the time to 10 minutes. Press the "Start" key.

2. In a mixing bowl, toss the fish with the other ingredients.

3. When the display indicates "Add Food", place the fish in the parchment-lined air fryer oven perforated pan.

4. Air fry the fish until it flakes easily with a fork. Bon appétit!

Nutrition:

- Info222 Calories,4.4g Fat,23.3g Carbs,19.8g Protei.

Spicy Jumbo Shrimp

Servings: 4

Cooking Time: 10 Minutes

Ingredients:

- 1/4 cup mayonnaise
- 1/2 cup all-purpose flour
- Sea salt and freshly ground black pepper, to taste
- 1 teaspoon ancho chile pepper
- 1 tablespoon brown mustard
- 1 cup seasoned breadcrumbs
- 1 pound jumbo shrimp, peeled and deveined

Directions:

1. In a shallow bowl, mix the mayonnaise, flour, salt, black pepper, ancho chile pepper, and brown mustard. In another shallow bowl, place the seasoned breadcrumbs.

2. Dredge the shrimp in the mayo mixture. Then, dip the strips in the breadcrumbs, coating them completely and shaking off any excess.

3. Select the "Air Fry" function and adjust the temperature to 390 degrees F. Press the "Start" key.

4. Arrange the shrimp on the air fryer oven perforated pan, making sure not to crowd them. Air fry the shrimp for 10 minutes or until it is thoroughly cooked. Enjoy!

Nutrition:

- Info153 Calories,4.4g Fat,4.2g Carbs,23.5g Protei.

Mediterranean Fish And Aioli Salad

Servings: 4

Cooking Time: 15 Minutes + Chilling Time

Ingredients:

- Salad:
- 1 pound codfish
- 1 teaspoon olive oil
- 1 tablespoon Cajun seasoning mix
- 1/2 cup cherry tomatoes
- 1/2 cup black olives, pitted
- 1 Greek cucumber, sliced
- 1 red onion, thinly sliced
- 1 bell pepper, thinly sliced
- Dressing:
- 1/4 cup aioli
- 2 tablespoons fresh lemon juice
- Sea salt and ground black pepper, to taste
- 1 tablespoon Dijon mustard
- 2 garlic cloves, crushed

Directions:

1. Select the "Air Fry" function and adjust the temperature to 400 degrees F. Set the oven to "Rotate" and set time to 10 minutes. Press the "Start" key.

2. In a mixing bowl, toss the fish with the olive oil and Cajun seasoning mix.

3. When the display indicates "Add Food", place the fish in the rotisserie basket.

4. Roast the fish until it is thoroughly cooked. Cut your fish into strips and place them in a salad bowl; add in the remaining salad ingredients and toss to combine.

5. Whisk all the dressing ingredients. Dress your salad and serve well-chilled. Enjoy!

Nutrition:

- Info255 Calories,17.4g Fat,6.6g Carbs,18.5g Protei.

Parmesan Salmon Croquettes

Servings: 4
Cooking Time: 15 Minutes
Ingredients:
- 12 ounces salmon fillets, chopped
- 2 garlic cloves, grated
- 1 small onion, chopped
- 1 teaspoon red pepper flakes, crushed
- 1 teaspoon dried oregano
- Kosher salt and black pepper, to taste
- 1 teaspoon lemon juice
- 1 large egg, beaten
- 1/2 cup tortilla chips, crushed
- 1/2 cup Parmesan cheese, grated
- 2 tablespoons butter

Directions:
1. Select the "Air Fry" function and adjust the temperature to 390 degrees F. Press the "Start" key.
2. Place a sheet of parchment paper in the air fryer oven pan. Thoroughly combine all the ingredients.
3. Form the mixture into equal balls and place them in a single layer in the air fryer oven perforated pan.
4. Air fry the croquettes for 12 minutes, turning them over halfway through.
5. Bon appétit!

Nutrition:
- Info285 Calories,16.6g Fat,8.3g Carbs,23.7g Protei.

Cajun Squid Rings

Servings: 4
Cooking Time: 15 Minutes
Ingredients:
- 1 pound squid rings
- 1 teaspoon onion powder
- 1 teaspoon garlic powder
- 1/2 cup spelt flour
- 1/2 cup buttermilk
- 1 teaspoon Cajun seasoning mix
- Sea salt and ground black pepper, to season
- 2 teaspoons olive oil

Directions:
1. In a mixing bowl, thoroughly combine all the ingredients, except for the squid rings.
2. Dredge the squid rings in the buttermilk mixture.
3. Select the "Air Fry" function and adjust the temperature to 390 degrees F. Press the "Start" key.
4. Arrange the squid rings on the air fryer oven perforated pan, making sure not to crowd them. Air fry the squid rings for 10 minutes or until golden brown.
5. Bon appétit!

Nutrition:
- Info215 Calories,4.1g Fat,21.6g Carbs,19.2g Protei.

Mini Smoked Salmon Frittatas

Servings: 4
Cooking Time: 15 Minutes
Ingredients:
- 12 ounces smoked salmon, chopped
- 6 eggs
- 1 ounce butter, softened
- 2 ounces cream cheese
- 1/4 cup sour cream
- 2 tablespoons fresh parsley, chopped
- 2 tablespoons fresh basil, chopped
- 2 tablespoons fresh scallions, chopped
- Sea salt and freshly ground black pepper, to season

Directions:
1. Select the "Bake" function and adjust the temperature to 350 degrees F and the time to 13 minutes. Press the "Start" key.
2. Meanwhile, brush silicone muffin cups with nonstick oil. Mix all the ingredients until well combined. Divide the mixture between the muffin cups.
3. When the display indicates "Add Food", place the muffin cups on the cooking tray in the center position.
4. Cook the mini fritters to your desired texture and serve warm. Bon appétit!

Nutrition:
- Info355 Calories,24.5g Fat,2.5g Carbs,27.3g Protei.

Cajun Crab Sticks

Servings: 4
Cooking Time: 15 Minutes
Ingredients:
- 1 pound crab sticks
- 1 teaspoon garlic, minced
- 1 tablespoon lemon juice
- 1 teaspoon Dijon mustard
- 1 tablespoon butter, melted
- 1 teaspoon Cajun seasoning mix
- Sea salt and ground black pepper, to taste

Directions:
1. Select the "Air Fry" function and adjust the temperature to 380 degrees F. Press the "Start" key.
2. In a mixing bowl, toss the crab sticks with the remaining ingredients.
3. When the display indicates "Add Food", place the crab sticks in the air fryer oven perforated pan.
4. Air fry the crab sticks for 12 minutes or until pink and opaque.
5. Bon appétit!

Nutrition:
- Info138 Calories,4.1g Fat,0.8g Carbs,20.5g Protei.

Greek-style Pita Wraps

Servings: 4
Cooking Time: 15 Minutes
Ingredients:
- 1 pound haddock fillets
- 2 ounces anchovy fillets
- 2 teaspoons olive oil
- 1/4 cup mayonnaise
- 2 ounces feta cheese, crumbled
- Sea salt and ground black pepper, to taste
- 2 cups mixed greens
- 1 red onion, thinly sliced
- 4 pita breads

Directions:
1. Select the "Air Fry" function and adjust the temperature to 400 degrees F. Set the oven to "Rotate" and set time to 10 minutes. Press the "Start" key.
2. Toss the fish with olive oil and place it in the rotisserie basket. Air fry the fish for 10 minutes or until it is thoroughly cooked.
3. Cut the fish into strips.
4. Assemble the pita wraps with warm fish strips and the remaining ingredients. Serve immediately and enjoy!

Nutrition:
- Info315 Calories,12.3g Fat,18.7g Carbs,28.7g Protei.

Fish Salad Sandwich

Servings: 4
Cooking Time: 15 Minutes
Ingredients:
- 1 pound ocean trout fillets
- 1 radicchio, trimmed and shredded
- 1 cucumber, sliced
- 1 bell pepper, sliced
- 1/4 cup extra-virgin olive oil
- 2 tablespoons fresh mint leaves, chopped
- 1 teaspoon garlic, minced
- 1 tablespoon lemon juice
- 1 tablespoon Dijon mustard
- 8 thin bread slices

Directions:
1. Select the "Air Fry" function and adjust the temperature to 400 degrees F. Set the oven to "Rotate" and set time to 10 minutes. Press the "Start" key.
2. When the display indicates "Add Food", place the fish in the rotisserie basket.

3. Roast the fish until it is thoroughly cooked. Cut your fish into strips and place them in a salad bowl; add in the vegetables, olive oil, mint, garlic, lemon juice, and mustard.
4. Assemble four sandwiches with bread slices and well-chilled salad. Enjoy!

Nutrition:
- Info325 Calories,16.2g Fat,22.2g Carbs,24g Protei.

Restaurant-style Calamari

Servings: 4
Cooking Time: 10 Minutes
Ingredients:
- 1/4 cup cream of onion soup
- 2 medium eggs, beaten
- 1/2 cup all-purpose flour
- 1/2 cup tortilla chips, crushed
- Sea salt and ground black pepper, to taste
- 1 teaspoon red pepper flakes, crushed
- 1 teaspoon garlic powder
- 2 teaspoon olive oil
- 1 pound squid rings

Directions:
1. In a shallow bowl, mix the soup, egg, and flour. In another shallow bowl, place tortilla chips, spices, and olive oil.
2. Dredge the squid rings in the egg mixture. Then, dip the squid rings in crushed tortilla chips, coating them completely.
3. Select the "Air Fry" function and adjust the temperature to 390 degrees F. Press the "Start" key.
4. Arrange the squid rings on the air fryer oven perforated pan, making sure not to crowd them. Air fry the squid rings for 10 minutes or until golden brown.
5. Bon appétit!

Nutrition:
- Info295 Calories,9.5g Fat,27.3g Carbs,23.5g Protei.

Mediterranean-style Shrimp Salad

Servings: 4
Cooking Time: 15 Minutes + Chilling Time
Ingredients:

- 1 pound shrimp, peeled and deveined
- 1/4 cup extra-virgin olive oil
- 1 teaspoon Dijon mustard
- 2 teaspoons lime juice
- Sea salt and freshly ground black pepper, to taste
- 1 small red onion, chopped
- 2 tablespoons fresh dill, chopped
- 2 tablespoons fresh parsley, chopped
- 2 cups Romaine lettuce

Directions:

1. Select the "Air Fry" function and adjust the temperature to 400 degrees F. Press the "Start" key.
2. In a mixing bowl, toss the shrimp with 1 teaspoon of olive oil.
3. When the display indicates "Add Food", place the shrimp in the air fryer oven perforated pan.
4. Air fry the shrimp for 7 to 8 minutes or until pink and opaque. Toss your shrimp with the other salad ingredients and serve well-chilled.
5. Bon appétit!

Nutrition:

- Info243 Calories,14.8g Fat,4.6g Carbs,23.9g Protei.

Favorite Seafood Sliders

Servings: 4
Cooking Time: 20 Minutes
Ingredients:

- 12 ounces shrimp, chopped
- 2 large eggs, whisked
- Zest of 1 lemon
- 1/2 cup seasoned breadcrumbs
- 1/2 cup parmesan cheese, preferably freshly grated
- 1 large onion, chopped
- 2 garlic cloves, minced
- 1/2 teaspoon dried oregano
- 1/2 teaspoon dried dill
- Kosher salt and freshly cracked black pepper, to taste
- 2 tablespoons olive oil
- 8 dinner rolls

Directions:

1. Select the "Air Fry" function and adjust the temperature to 390 degrees F. Press the "Start" key.
2. Place a sheet of parchment paper in the air fryer oven pan. Thoroughly combine all the ingredients, except for the dinner rolls.
3. Form the mixture into eight patties and place them in a single layer in the air fryer oven perforated pan.
4. Air fry the patties for 15 minutes, turning them over halfway through. Assemble your slider with warm patties and dinner rolls and serve immediately.
5. Bon appétit!

Nutrition:

- Info415 Calories,16.9g Fat,36.5g Carbs,29.7g Protei.

Paprika Shrimp Salad

Servings: 4
Cooking Time: 10 Minutes + Chilling Time
Ingredients:

- 1 pound shrimp, peeled and chilled
- 2 stalks celery, diced
- 1 red onion, chopped
- 2 garlic cloves, minced
- 2 hard-boiled eggs, peeled and diced
- 1 small cucumber, sliced
- 1 tablespoon fresh dill, minced
- 1/2 cup mayonnaise
- 1 tablespoon Dijon mustard
- 1 teaspoon paprika
- Kosher salt and ground black pepper, to taste

Directions:

1. Select the "Air Fry" function and adjust the temperature to 400 degrees F. Press the "Start" key.
2. In a mixing bowl, toss the shrimp with the remaining ingredients.
3. When the display indicates "Add Food", place the shrimp in the air fryer oven perforated pan. Air fry the shrimp for 7 to 8 minutes or until pink and opaque.
4. Toss your shrimp with the other salad ingredients and serve well-chilled.
5. Bon appétit!

Nutrition:

- Info352 Calories,24.4g Fat,5.2g Carbs,27g Protei.

Halibut Taco Wraps

Servings: 4
Cooking Time: 15 Minutes
Ingredients:
- 1 pound halibut fillets
- 2 teaspoon olive oil
- 1 teaspoon ancho chili powder
- 1/2 cup salsa, preferably homemade
- 1 ½ cups coleslaw mix
- 4 large corn tortillas (or flour tortillas)

Directions:
1. Select the "Air Fry" function and adjust the temperature to 400 degrees F. Set the oven to "Rotate" and set time to 10 minutes. Press the "Start" key.
2. Toss the fish with olive oil and chili powder; place the fish in the rotisserie basket. Air fry the fish for 10 minutes or until it is thoroughly cooked.
3. Cut the fish into strips.
4. Assemble your taco wraps with warm fish strips, salsa, coleslaw, and tortillas. Serve immediately and enjoy!

Nutrition:
- Info480 Calories,22.4g Fat,36.3g Carbs,22.6g Protei.

Grilled Flatbread Sandwiches

Servings: 4
Cooking Time: 10 Minutes
Ingredients:
- 4 slices Colby cheese
- 8 ounces canned tuna, drained
- 1 tablespoon Dijon mustard
- 4 heaping tablespoons mayonnaise
- 1/2 cup dill pickles, thinly sliced
- 1 bell pepper, seeded and sliced
- 4 large flour tortillas

Directions:
1. Assemble your sandwich with tortillas and other ingredients; you can use a toothpick to keep the sandwich together.
2. When the display indicates "Add Food", place the sandwich on the air fryer tray.
3. Select the "Toast" function and press the "Start" key.
4. Toast the sandwich for about 3 minutes or so. Serve immediately.

Nutrition:
- Info425 Calories,18g Fat,39.4g Carbs,24.5g Protei.

Favorite Seafood Fritters

Servings: 4
Cooking Time: 15 Minutes
Ingredients:
- 1 pound shrimp, peeled and deveined
- 1 large sweet onion, chopped
- 1 teaspoon garlic, pressed
- 1 bell pepper, chopped
- 1/2 cup all-purpose flour
- 1/2 cup tortilla chips, crushed
- 2 teaspoons butter, melted
- 1 teaspoon baking powder
- 1 teaspoon Cajun seasoning mix
- Sea salt and freshly ground black pepper, to taste
- 1 teaspoon paprika
- 1 teaspoon stone-ground mustard
- 2 large eggs, beaten
- ¼ cup cream of celery soup

Directions:
1. Select the "Air Fry" function and adjust the temperature to 370 degrees F. Press the "Start" key.
2. Place a sheet of parchment paper in the air fryer oven pan.
3. Thoroughly combine all the ingredients in a mixing bowl. Form the mixture into equal patties and place them in a single layer in the air fryer oven perforated pan.
4. Air fry the fritters for 13 minutes. Serve warm and enjoy!

Nutrition:
- Info345 Calories,10.4g Fat,32.8g Carbs,30.1g Protei.

Roasted Salmon With Cauliflower

Servings: 4
Cooking Time: 15 Minutes
Ingredients:
- 1 pound salmon steaks
- 1 pound cauliflower florets
- 1 teaspoon garlic powder
- 1 teaspoon onion powder
- 1/2 teaspoon turmeric powder
- 2 tablespoons olive oil
- Sea salt and ground black pepper, to taste
- Juice of 1 lemon

Directions:
1. Select the "Air Fry" function and adjust the temperature to 400 degrees F. Press the "Start" key.
2. When the display indicates "Add Food", toss all the ingredients into the air fryer oven perforated pan.
3. Roast the salmon and cauliflower for 10 minutes or until cooked through. Serve warm and enjoy!

Nutrition:
- Info285 Calories,13.9g Fat,8.8g Carbs,32.5g Protei.

Sea Scallop Sandwiches

Servings: 4

Cooking Time: 15 Minutes

Ingredients:

- 1 pound sea scallops
- 2 tablespoons fresh lemon juice
- 2 teaspoons olive oil
- 2 spring onions, cut in half
- 1/4 cup mayonnaise
- 1 tablespoon Dijon mustard
- Sea salt and freshly ground black pepper, to taste
- 1 cup fresh arugula
- 4 hamburger buns

Directions:

1. Select the "Air Fry" function and adjust the temperature to 400 degrees F. Press the "Start" key.

2. When the display indicates "Add Food", toss the sea scallops with the fresh lemon juice and olive oil; place them in the air fryer oven perforated pan.

3. Air fry the sea scallops for 10 minutes or until pink and opaque.

4. Assemble your sandwiches with the fried scallops, onions, mayonnaise, mustard, salt, black pepper, arugula, and hamburger buns.

5. Bon appétit!

Nutrition:

- Info326 Calories,14.4g Fat,26.1g Carbs,18.4g Protei.

Street-style Fish Fritters

Servings: 5

Cooking Time: 15 Minutes

Ingredients:

- 1 ½ pounds haddock, chopped (or any other mild white fish)
- 2 ounces bacon bits
- 1 zucchini, grated
- 1 medium onion, diced
- 2 garlic cloves, minced
- 1 chili pepper, chopped
- 2 medium eggs, beaten
- ¼ cup full-fat milk
- 1 cup instant oats
- 1 teaspoon baking powder

Directions:

1. Select the "Air Fry" function and adjust the temperature to 390 degrees F. Press the "Start" key.

2. Place a sheet of parchment paper in the air fryer oven pan. Thoroughly combine all the ingredients.

3. Form the mixture into four patties and place them in a single layer in the air fryer oven perforated pan.

4. Air fry the patties for 12 minutes, turning them over halfway through. Serve warm and enjoy!

Nutrition:

- Info315 Calories,9.4g Fat,24.8g Carbs,32.2g Protei.

Hot Sardine Cutlets

Servings: 4

Cooking Time: 15 Minutes

Ingredients:

- 10 ounces sardines, drained and chopped
- 1 large egg, well-beaten
- 1 tablespoon ground chia seeds
- 1 medium onion, chopped
- 2 garlic cloves, minced
- 1 carrot, grated
- 2 tablespoons butter, softened
- 2 tablespoons mayonnaise
- 1 teaspoon Sriracha sauce
- Kosher salt and ground black pepper, to season
- 1 teaspoon smoked paprika
- 1/2 cup seasoned breadcrumbs

Directions:

1. Select the "Air Fry" function and adjust the temperature to 390 degrees F. Press the "Start" key.

2. Place a sheet of parchment paper in the air fryer oven pan. Thoroughly combine all the ingredients.

3. Form the mixture into equal patties and place them in a single layer in the air fryer oven perforated pan.

4. Air fry the patties for 13 minutes, turning them over halfway through.

5. Bon appétit!

Nutrition:

- Info320 Calories,17.6g Fat,16.3g Carbs,20.3g Protei.

Garlicky Flounder Fillets

Servings: 4
Cooking Time: 15 Minutes
Ingredients:

- 1 ½ pounds flounder fillets
- 2 garlic cloves, minced
- 1/2 cup parmesan cheese, preferably freshly grated
- 1 cup crackers, crushed
- 2 tablespoons oil
- 1 teaspoon dried parsley flakes
- 1 teaspoon dried basil
- 1 teaspoon dried oregano
- 2 medium eggs, well-beaten

Directions:

1. Select the "Air Fry" function and adjust the temperature to 400 degrees F. Set the time to 10 minutes. Press the "Start" key.
2. In a mixing bowl, toss the fish with the other ingredients.
3. When the display indicates "Add Food", place the fish in the parchment-lined air fryer oven perforated pan.
4. Air fry the fish until it flakes easily with a fork. Bon appétit!

Nutrition:

- Info395 Calories,22.2g Fat,17.9g Carbs,29.1g Protei.

Creole Catfish Fillets

Servings: 4
Cooking Time: 15 Minutes
Ingredients:

- 1 pound catfish fillets
- 2 eggs, beaten
- 1/2 cup all-purpose flour
- 1/2 cup breadcrumbs
- 1 teaspoon Creole seasoning mix
- 2 teaspoons olive oil
- 1 tablespoon fresh parsley, chopped
- 1 tablespoon fresh cilantro, chopped

Directions:

1. Select the "Air Fry" function and adjust the temperature to 400 degrees F. Set the time to 10 minutes. Press the "Start" key.
2. Pat the fish dry. In a shallow bowl, whisk the eggs with the flour. In a shallow bowl, mix the remaining ingredients.
3. Dip the fish into the egg mixture. Then, roll the fish over the breadcrumb mixture.
4. When the display indicates "Add Food", place the fish in the parchment-lined air fryer oven perforated pan.
5. Air fry the fish until it flakes easily with a fork. Bon appétit!

Nutrition:

- Info244 Calories,7.8g Fat,15.4g Carbs,23.5g Protei.

Pork And Beef Recipes

Bbq Back Ribs

Servings: 4
Cooking Time: 45 Minutes
Ingredients:

- 2 pounds baby back pork ribs
- 1/2 cup barbeque sauce
- 1 teaspoon ancho chile powder
- 1/4 cup brown sugar
- Sea salt and freshly ground black pepper, to taste

Directions:

1. Select the "Air Fry" function and adjust the temperature to 350 degrees F. Press the "Start" key.
2. Toss the pork ribs with the other ingredients. Place aluminum foil onto the drip pan.
3. When the display indicates "Add Food", add the pork ribs to the rotisserie basket. Cook the pork ribs for about 40 minutes or until they are thoroughly cooked.
4. Bon appétit!

Nutrition:

- Info352 Calories,12.9g Fat,8.5g Carbs,47.6g Protei.

Restaurant-style Hamburgers

Servings: 4
Cooking Time: 30 Minutes
Ingredients:
- 1 pound ground chuck
- Kosher salt and ground black pepper, to taste
- 1 teaspoon cayenne pepper
- 1 small onion, chopped
- 2 garlic cloves, minced
- 1 chili pepper, minced
- 4 hamburger buns
- 8 lettuce leaves
- 2 teaspoons yellow mustard
- 4 teaspoons mayonnaise

Directions:
1. Select the "Air Fry" function and adjust the temperature to 390 degrees F. Press the "Start" key.
2. Place a sheet of parchment paper in the air fryer oven pan.
3. Mix the ground chuck, salt, black pepper, cayenne pepper, onion, garlic, and chili pepper until well combined.
4. Shape the mixture into four patties and place them in a single layer in the air fryer oven perforated pan.
5. Air fry your hamburgers for 25 minutes. Assemble your hamburgers with warm patties, hamburger buns, lettuce, mustard, and mayo.
6. Bon appétit!

Nutrition:
- Info375 Calories,17.8g Fat,25.8g Carbs,27.3g Protei.

Cheesy Loaded Meatloaf

Servings: 5
Cooking Time: 30 Minutes
Ingredients:
- Meatloaf:
- 1 ½ pounds ground beef
- 1 medium onion, chopped ed
- 2 garlic cloves, pressed
- 2 eggs, beaten
- 1 teaspoon paprika
- Sea salt and ground black pepper, to taste
- ½ cup seasoned bread crumbs
- ½ cup parmesan cheese, grated
- 2 teaspoons soy sauce
- 1 teaspoon oregano
- 1 teaspoon rosemary
- Glaze:
- 1 cup tomato sauce
- 2 tablespoons brown sugar

Directions:
1. Thoroughly combine all the ingredients for the meatloaf; press the meatloaf into a lightly greased baking pan.
2. Select the "Air Fry" function and adjust the temperature to 400 degrees F. Press the "Start" key.
3. When the display indicates "Add Food", add the baking pan to the cooking tray. Air fry the meatloaf for 20 minutes.
4. Mix the glaze ingredients and spread the mixture over the top of your meatloaf.
5. Select the "Broil" function and cook the meatloaf for 5 minutes more. Bon appétit!

Nutrition:
- Info480 Calories,25.5g Fat,24.4g Carbs,37.1g Protei.

Herbed Ribeye Steak

Servings: 4
Cooking Time: 20 Minutes + Marinating Time
Ingredients:
- 1 pound ribeye steak, cut into cubes
- 2 tablespoons apple cider vinegar
- 1 teaspoon paprika
- Sea salt and freshly cracked black pepper, to taste
- 2 tablespoons olive oil
- 2 tablespoons fresh parsley, chopped
- 2 tablespoons fresh cilantro, chopped
- 2 tablespoons fresh basil, chopped
- 2 garlic cloves, minced
- 2 tablespoons Worcestershire sauce

Directions:
1. Add all the ingredients to a ceramic or glass bowl. Allow the beef to marinate for at least 3 hours.
2. Select the "Air Fry" function and adjust the temperature to 365 degrees F. Press the "Start" key. Place aluminum foil onto the drip pan.
3. When the display indicates "Add Food", place the beef in the air fryer oven perforated pan. Reserve the marinade. Cook the beef for about 12 minutes.
4. Increase the temperature of the oven to 400 degrees F; baste the beef with the reserved marinade and continue to cook for 5 to 6 minutes more.
5. Serve warm and enjoy!

Nutrition:
- Info335 Calories,25.9g Fat,3.7g Carbs,21.9g Protei.

Chuck Roast With Brussels Sprouts

Servings: 5
Cooking Time: 35 Minutes + Marinating Time
Ingredients:

- 1 ½ pounds chuck roast
- 1 teaspoon garlic, minced
- 1 teaspoon cayenne pepper
- 2 tablespoons rice vinegar
- 2 tablespoons soy sauce
- 1 tablespoon Dijon mustard
- 1 pound Brussels sprouts
- 2 tablespoons butter, at room temperature
- 1 teaspoon dried thyme
- 1 teaspoon dried rosemary

Directions:

1. Place the beef, garlic, cayenne pepper, vinegar, soy sauce, and mustard in a ceramic or glass bowl. Allow the beef to marinate for at least 3 hours.
2. Select the "Air Fry" function and adjust the temperature to 390 degrees F. Press the "Start" key. Place aluminum foil onto the drip pan.
3. When the display indicates "Add Food", place the beef in the air fryer oven perforated pan. Reserve the marinade. Cook the beef for about 15 minutes.
4. Add in the remaining ingredients, baste the beef with the reserved marinade and continue to cook for 15 minutes longer.
5. Bon appétit!

Nutrition:

- Info369 Calories,24.2g Fat,10.3g Carbs,29.8g Protei.

Favorite Pork Salad

Servings: 4
Cooking Time: 50 Minutes
Ingredients:

- 1 pound pork loin
- 3 cups mixed salad greens, torn into pieces
- 1 cup grape tomatoes
- 1 small red onion, thinly sliced
- 1 bell pepper, sliced
- 1 small chili pepper, minced
- 1/4 cup extra-virgin olive oil
- 2 tablespoons apple cider vinegar
- 2 teaspoons fresh basil, minced
- 1 teaspoon fish sauce
- 2 garlic cloves, minced

Directions:

1. Select the "Roast" function and adjust the temperature to 360 degrees F. Press the "Start" key. Place aluminum foil onto the drip pan.
2. When the display indicates "Add Food", place the pork loin in the air fryer oven perforated pan. Cook the pork for about 25 minutes.
3. Turn the pork over and continue to roast for about 20 minutes or until it reaches an internal temperature of 145 degrees F on a meat thermometer.
4. Cut the pork into strips and place them in a salad bowl. Add in the vegetables and toss to combine. Whisk the remaining ingredients to make the dressing.
5. Dress your salad and enjoy!

Nutrition:

- Info368 Calories,23.3g Fat,13.3g Carbs,26.5g Protei.

Beef Eye Round Roast

Servings: 5
Cooking Time: 50 Minutes
Ingredients:

- 2 pounds beef eye round roast
- 2 tablespoons olive oil
- 2 garlic cloves, pressed
- 1 teaspoon dried basil
- 1 teaspoon dried oregano
- 1 teaspoon dried rosemary
- 1 teaspoon red pepper flakes, crushed
- Sea salt and ground black pepper, to taste

Directions:

1. Select the "Roast" function and adjust the temperature to 360 degrees F. Set the oven to "Rotate" and set the time to 45 minutes. Press the "Start" key.
2. Pat the beef dry. Rub olive oil, garlic, and spices all over the round roast.
3. When the display indicates "Add Food", place the beef in the rotisserie basket.
4. Roast the beef until it reaches an internal temperature of 160 degrees F on a meat thermometer.
5. Bon appétit!

Nutrition:

- Info393 Calories,20.9g Fat,0.6g Carbs,48.5g Protei.

Korean-style Steak Cubes

Servings: 5
Cooking Time: 20 Minutes + Marinating Time
Ingredients:

- 1 pound top round steak, cut into bite-sized cubes
- 2 tablespoons rice vinegar
- 2 tablespoons toasted sesame oil
- 1 teaspoon stone-ground mustard
- 2 tablespoons soy sauce
- 4 cloves garlic, crushed
- 1 teaspoon ginger, peeled and minced
- 1/4 cup brown sugar
- Sea salt and crushed red pepper, to taste
- 1 pound broccoli florets
- 2 bell peppers, sliced
- 1 medium onion, cut into wedges

Directions:

1. Add the steak, vinegar, sesame oil, mustard, soy sauce, garlic, ginger, sugar, salt, and red pepper to a ceramic or glass bowl. Allow the beef to marinate for 3 hours.
2. Select the "Air Fry" function and adjust the temperature to 365 degrees F. Press the "Start" key. Place aluminum foil onto the drip pan.
3. When the display indicates "Add Food", place the steak and vegetables in the air fryer oven perforated pan. Cook the steak cubes for about 8 minutes, turning it twice during the cooking time.
4. Increase temperature to 400 degrees F and continue cooking for 8 minutes more.

Nutrition:

- Info317 Calories,12.4g Fat,18.3g Carbs,32.7g Protei.

Memphis-style Beef Back Ribs

Servings: 4
Cooking Time: 20 Minutes
Ingredients:

- 1 ½ pounds beef back ribs
- 1 cup BBQ sauce
- Kosher salt and freshly ground black pepper, to taste
- 1 tablespoon brown sugar
- 1 tablespoon brown mustard
- 1 teaspoon hot paprika
- 1 teaspoon garlic powder
- 1 teaspoon onion powder

Directions:

1. Add all the ingredients to a ceramic or glass bowl. Allow the beef to marinate for at least 3 hours.
2. Select the "Air Fry" function and adjust the temperature to 360 degrees F. Press the "Start" key. Place aluminum foil onto the drip pan.
3. When the display indicates "Add Food", place the beef ribs in the air fryer oven perforated pan. Reserve the marinade. Cook the beef for about 15 minutes.
4. Serve immediately and enjoy!

Nutrition:

- Info412 Calories,28g Fat,8.2g Carbs,34.3g Protei.

Juicy And Tender Beef Roast

Servings: 6
Cooking Time: 50 Minutes + Marinating Time
Ingredients:

- 2 ½ pounds beef roast
- 2 tablespoons olive oil
- 1/4 cup wine vinegar
- 1 tablespoon mustard
- 1 teaspoon dried thyme
- 1 teaspoon garlic powder
- 1 teaspoon onion powder
- 1 teaspoon turmeric powder
- 1 teaspoon cayenne pepper
- Sea salt and ground black pepper, to taste

Directions:

1. Place all the ingredients in a ceramic bowl. Cover and let it marinate for at least 1 hour.
2. Select the "Roast" function and adjust the temperature to 360 degrees F. Press the "Start" key.
3. Now, grease the air fryer oven perforated pan with nonstick spray.
4. When the display indicates "Add Food", place the beef in the air fryer oven perforated pan. Reserve the marinade. Roast for 20 minutes in the preheated air fryer oven.
5. Turn the roast over, baste with the reserved marinade, and roast for a further 30 minutes for medium-rare. You can roast your beef for 20 minutes more or until it is well-done.
6. Bon appétit!

Nutrition:

- Info303 Calories,15.5g Fat,1.4g Carbs,39.2g Protei.

Italian-style Pulled Pork

Servings: 5
Cooking Time: 55 Minutes + Marinating Time
Ingredients:

- 2 pounds boneless pork shoulder
- 1 tablespoon Italian seasoning mix
- 1/2 teaspoon cumin seeds
- 2 garlic cloves, pressed
- Sea salt and ground black pepper, to taste
- 1 teaspoon hot paprika

Directions:

1. Add all the ingredients to a ceramic or glass bowl. Allow the pork to marinate for at least 3 hours.
2. Select the "Air Fry" function and adjust the temperature to 360 degrees F. Press the "Start" key. Place aluminum foil onto the drip pan.
3. When the display indicates "Add Food", place the pork in the air fryer oven perforated pan. Reserve the marinade. Cook the pork for about 25 minutes.
4. Baste the pork with the reserved marinade and continue to roast for about 25 minutes or until cooked through. Shred the pork with two forks and serve immediately.
5. Bon appétit!

Nutrition:

- Info346 Calories,22.5g Fat,1.4g Carbs,31.8g Protei.

Hot And Spicy Ribs

Servings: 5
Cooking Time: 40 Minutes
Ingredients:

- 2 pounds Country-style pork ribs
- 1 teaspoon paprika
- 2 teaspoons garlic powder
- 1 teaspoon dried thyme
- Sea salt and ground black pepper
- 1/4 cup apple cider
- 2 tablespoons olive oil
- 1 cup tomato sauce
- 2 tablespoons molasses
- 1 tablespoon mustard powder
- 1 teaspoon Tabasco

Directions:

1. Place all the ingredients in a ceramic dish. Let it marinate for at least 1 hour.
2. Select the "Air Fry" function and adjust the temperature to 350 degrees F. Press the "Start" key. Place aluminum foil onto the drip pan.

3. When the display indicates "Add Food", add the pork ribs to the rotisserie basket. Cook the pork ribs for about 35 minutes or until they are thoroughly cooked.
4. Bon appétit!
Nutrition:

- Info396 Calories,16.1g Fat,19.6g Carbs,36.9g Protei.

Beef Brisket Salad

Servings: 4
Cooking Time: 50 Minutes
Ingredients:

- 1 pound beef brisket
- 2 green onions, chopped
- 1 garlic clove, minced
- 1/4 cup fresh mint leaves, chopped
- 1/4 cup fresh lime juice
- 1 teaspoon sweet chili sauce
- 1 head Romaine lettuce, torn into bite-size pieces
- 1 medium cucumber, diced
- 1 cup grape tomatoes, halved
- 1 bell pepper, sliced

Directions:

1. Select the "Air Fry" function and adjust the temperature to 350 degrees F. Press the "Start" key.
2. Toss the beef brisket with the other ingredients. Place aluminum foil onto the drip pan.
3. When the display indicates "Add Food", place the beef in the air fryer oven perforated pan. Cook the beef brisket for about 25 minutes.
4. Turn the temperature to 390 degrees F. Turn it over and continue to cook for 25 minutes more.
5. Slice the beef into strips and toss it with the remaining ingredients.
6. Serve your salad at room temperature and enjoy!
Nutrition:

- Info347 Calories,22.5g Fat,13.2g Carbs,23.9g Protei.

Teriyaki Beef Brisket

Servings: 4
Cooking Time: 55 Minutes
Ingredients:

- 1 ½ pounds beef brisket, boneless
- 2 tablespoons agave nectar
- 2 garlic cloves, minced
- 1 teaspoon chili powder
- 1 teaspoon mustard powder
- Sea salt and ground black pepper, to taste
- 1/4 cup teriyaki sauce

Directions:

1. Select the "Air Fry" function and adjust the temperature to 350 degrees F. Press the "Start" key.
2. Toss the beef with the other ingredients. Place aluminum foil onto the drip pan.
3. When the display indicates "Add Food", place the beef in the air fryer oven perforated pan. Cook the beef for about 25 minutes.
4. Turn the temperature to 390 degrees F. Turn it over and continue to cook for 25 minutes more.
5. Serve warm and enjoy!

Nutrition:

- Info377 Calories,25.4g Fat,6.2g Carbs,26.3g Protei.

Steak And Avocado Salad

Servings: 5
Cooking Time: 20 Minutes + Marinating Time
Ingredients:

- 1 ½ pounds flank steak
- 1 tablespoon brown mustard
- 2 tablespoons red wine
- 4 tablespoons balsamic vinegar
- 1 red onion, sliced
- 1 bell pepper, sliced
- 1 garlic clove, minced
- 1 cucumber, diced
- 2 tablespoons extra-virgin olive oil
- Kosher salt and freshly ground black pepper
- 1 large tomato, diced
- 1 cup baby arugula
- 1 ripe avocado, peeled, pitted and sliced
- 1/4 cup pine nuts, toasted

Directions:

1. Add the steak mustard, red wine, and balsamic vinegar to a ceramic or glass bowl. Allow the beef to marinate for at least 2 hours.

2. Select the "Air Fry" function and adjust the temperature to 400 degrees F. Press the "Start" key. Place aluminum foil onto the drip pan.
3. When the display indicates "Add Food", place the steak in the air fryer oven perforated pan. Cook the steak for about 15 minutes, turning it twice during the cooking time.
4. Slice the steak into strips and add in the remaining ingredients; toss to combine. Serve the salad at room temperature and enjoy!

Nutrition:

- Info387 Calories,24.4g Fat,10.3g Carbs,31.7g Protei.

Blue Cheese-crusted Filet Mignon

Servings: 4
Cooking Time: 20 Minutes + Marinating Time
Ingredients:

- 1 ½ pounds fillet mignon
- 1 large egg, whisked
- 1 cup breadcrumbs
- 1 cup blue cheese, crumbled
- 2 tablespoons olive oil
- 1 garlic clove, minced
- 2 tablespoons fresh parsley, minced
- Coarse sea salt and ground black pepper, to taste

Directions:

1. Select the "Roast" function and adjust the temperature to 365 degrees F. Press the "Start" key.
2. Whisk the egg in a shallow bowl; in another shallow bowl, mix the remaining ingredients.
3. Dip the filet mignon into the whisked egg. Roll it into the cheese/crumb mixture.
4. When the display indicates "Add Food", place the beef in the air fryer oven perforated pan. Cook your fillet mignon for about 12 minutes.
5. Serve warm and enjoy!

Nutrition:

- Info473 Calories,28.1g Fat,7.8g Carbs,45.2g Protei.

Jalapeno Lime Skirt Steak

Servings: 4
Cooking Time: 20 Minutes + Marinating Time
Ingredients:

- 1 ½ pounds skirt steak
- 2 tablespoons soy sauce
- 1/2 cup red wine vinegar
- 2 tablespoons olive oil
- 2 tablespoons lime juice
- 1 jalapeno pepper, chopped
- 1 teaspoon cayenne pepper
- Sea salt and ground black pepper, to taste

Directions:

1. Add all the ingredients to a ceramic or glass bowl. Allow the beef to marinate for at least 3 hours.
2. Select the "Air Fry" function and adjust the temperature to 390 degrees F. Press the "Start" key. Place aluminum foil onto the drip pan.
3. When the display indicates "Add Food", place the beef in the air fryer oven perforated pan. Reserve the marinade. Cook the beef for about 12 minutes.
4. Increase the temperature of the oven to 400 degrees F; baste the beef with the reserved marinade and continue to cook for 5 to 6 minutes more.
5. Serve warm and enjoy!

Nutrition:

- Info467 Calories,28.7g Fat,3.1g Carbs,45.1g Protei.

Festive Baked Ham

Servings: 6
Cooking Time: 3 Hours
Ingredients:

- 2 pounds cooked boneless ham
- 1/2 cup brown sugar
- 2 tablespoons whole-grain mustard
- 1/2 cup sherry wine
- 2 tablespoons olive oil
- 2 garlic cloves, minced
- 2 tablespoons Worcestershire sauce

Directions:

1. Pat the ham dry.
2. Select the "Air Fry" function and adjust the temperature to 250 degrees F. Select the "Rotate" function, and set the time to 3 hours. Press the "Start" key.
3. When the display indicates "Add Food", place the prepared ham with the rotisserie spit into the oven.

4. Meanwhile, mix all the remaining ingredients to make the glaze. When the ham has reached 145 degrees F, brush the glaze over all surfaces of the ham.
5. Allow it to rest for 10 minutes before slicing and serving.
6. Bon appétit!

Nutrition:

- Info338 Calories,17.6g Fat,17.3g Carbs,25.4g Protei.

Pork Sirloin Sandwich

Servings: 4
Cooking Time: 50 Minutes
Ingredients:

- 1 pound pork sirloin
- 2 tablespoons olive oil
- 2 tablespoons soy sauce
- 2 garlic cloves, pressed
- 2 teaspoons brown sugar
- 2 teaspoons brown mustard
- Sea salt and cayenne pepper, to taste
- 4 Kaiser rolls, split
- 4 lettuce leaves
- 1 medium tomato, sliced

Directions:

1. Select the "Roast" function and adjust the temperature to 360 degrees F. Press the "Start" key. Place aluminum foil onto the drip pan.
2. Toss the pork with olive oil, soy sauce, garlic, sugar, mustard, salt, and cayenne pepper.
3. When the display indicates "Add Food", place the loin in the air fryer oven perforated pan. Cook the pork for about 25 minutes.
4. Turn the pork over and continue roasting for about 20 minutes or until it reaches an internal temperature of 145 degrees F on a meat thermometer.
5. Assemble your sandwiches with Kaiser rolls, lettuce, and tomato. Bon appétit!

Nutrition:

- Info456 Calories,22g Fat,35.2g Carbs,29g Protei.

New York Strip Steaks

Servings: 4
Cooking Time: 20 Minutes + Marinating Time
Ingredients:
- 1 ½ pounds New York strip steaks
- 2 teaspoons olive oil
- 2 tablespoons fresh lemon juice
- 1 tablespoon Dijon mustard
- Sea salt and ground black pepper, to taste
- 2 tablespoons fresh chives, chopped
- 2 tablespoons fresh parsley, chopped

Directions:
1. Add all the ingredients to a ceramic or glass bowl. Allow the beef to marinate for at least 1 hour.
2. Select the "Air Fry" function and adjust the temperature to 380 degrees F. Press the "Start" key. Place aluminum foil onto the drip pan.
3. When the display indicates "Add Food", place the beef in the air fryer oven perforated pan. Reserve the marinade. Cook the beef for about 12 minutes.
4. Increase the temperature of the oven to 400 degrees F; baste the beef with the reserved marinade and continue to cook for 5 to 6 minutes more.
5. Serve warm and enjoy!

Nutrition:
- Info292 Calories,9.1g Fat,2g Carbs,50.2g Protei.

Top Sirloin Petite Roast

Servings: 4
Cooking Time: 50 Minutes
Ingredients:
- 1 ½ pounds top sirloin petite roast, boneless
- 1 cup apple juice
- 2 cloves garlic, peeled and minced
- 1 teaspoon fresh thyme, finely chopped
- 1 teaspoon fresh rosemary, finely chopped
- 2 tablespoons fresh parsley, finely chopped
- 1 teaspoon paprika
- Sea salt and ground black pepper, to taste

Directions:
1. Select the "Roast" function and adjust the temperature to 360 degrees F. Press the "Start" key. Place aluminum foil onto the drip pan.
2. Toss the pork loin with the remaining ingredients.
3. When the display indicates "Add Food", place the pork loin in the air fryer oven perforated pan. Cook the pork for about 25 minutes.
4. Turn it over and continue to roast for about 20 minutes or until it reaches an internal temperature of 145 degrees F on a meat thermometer.
5. Serve immediately and enjoy!

Nutrition:
- Info378 Calories,21.6g Fat,9.1g Carbs,35.8g Protei.

Herbed Roast Beef

Servings: 6
Cooking Time: 45 Minutes
Ingredients:
- 2 pounds roast beef
- 2 tablespoons olive oil
- 2 cloves garlic, minced
- 1 teaspoon fresh rosemary, chopped
- 1 teaspoon fresh basil, chopped
- 1 teaspoon fresh thyme, chopped
- 1 teaspoon cayenne pepper
- Kosher salt and ground black pepper, to taste

Directions:
1. Select the "Air Fry" function and adjust the temperature to 360 degrees F. Press the "Start" key.
2. Pat the roast dry. Now, grease the air fryer oven perforated pan with olive oil.
3. When the display indicates "Add Food", place the beef in the air fryer oven perforated pan. Roast for 25 minutes in the preheated air fryer oven.
4. Turn the roast over and roast for additional 20 minutes.
5. Bon appétit!

Nutrition:
- Info325 Calories,17.3g Fat,0.6g Carbs,40g Protei.

Old-fashioned Mini Meatloaves

Servings: 4
Cooking Time: 30 Minutes
Ingredients:
- 1 pound ground pork
- 1 small carrot, grated
- 1 small bell pepper, chopped
- 1 cup tortilla chips, crushed
- 1 small shallot, chopped
- 1 teaspoon garlic, minced
- 1 egg, whisked

Directions:
1. Select the "Air Fry" function and adjust the temperature to 390 degrees F and the time to 25 minutes. Press the "Start" key.
2. Meanwhile, brush silicone muffin cups with nonstick cooking oil. Mix all the ingredients until well combined. Divide the mixture between the muffin cups.
3. When the display indicates "Add Food", place the muffin cups on the cooking tray.
4. Bake the mini meatloaves in the preheated air fryer oven until cooked through. Bon appétit!

Nutrition:
- Info425 Calories,25.9g Fat,23.7g Carbs,24.2g Protei.

Loaded Meatballs With Olives And Bacon

Servings: 4
Cooking Time: 25 Minutes
Ingredients:
- 1 pound ground pork
- 1/2 cup plain breadcrumbs
- 1 large egg, whisked
- 1 garlic clove, minced
- 1 teaspoon dried basil
- 1 teaspoon dried oregano
- Kosher salt and ground black pepper, to taste
- 1 teaspoon paprika
- 2 ounces bacon bits
- 2 ounces green olives, pitted and chopped

Directions:
1. Select the "Air Fry" function and adjust the temperature to 380 degrees F. Press the "Start" key.
2. Place a sheet of parchment paper in the air fryer oven pan.
3. In a mixing bowl, thoroughly combine all the ingredients. Then, drop rounds of the mixture in a single layer onto the prepared pan using a small scoop.
4. Air fry the meatballs for 10 minutes. Turn them over and continue cooking for a further 10 minutes or until cooked through.
5. Bon appétit!

Nutrition:
- Info436 Calories,36.6g Fat,4.5g Carbs,22.6g Protei.

Pork Belly With Brussels Sprouts

Servings: 5
Cooking Time: 20 Minutes
Ingredients:
- 1 pound pork belly cubes
- 1 pound Brussels sprouts
- 1 tablespoon brown sugar
- 1 teaspoon onion powder
- 1 teaspoon garlic powder
- 1/2 teaspoon ground cumin
- 1 teaspoon red pepper flakes, crushed
- Kosher salt and ground black pepper, to season

Directions:
1. Select the "Air Fry" function and adjust the temperature to 390 degrees F. Press the "Start" key. Place aluminum foil onto the drip pan.
2. Toss all the ingredients in a mixing bowl.
3. When the display indicates "Add Food", place the pork and Brussels sprouts in the air fryer oven perforated pan.
4. Cook the pork and Brussels sprouts for about 10 minutes. Turn over and continue to cook for a further 8 minutes.
5. Serve immediately and enjoy!

Nutrition:
- Info521 Calories,48.1g Fat,10.7g Carbs,11.7g Protei.

Italian-style Meatloaf

Servings: 5
Cooking Time: 45 Minutes
Ingredients:
- Meatloaf:
- 1 ½ pounds ground pork
- 1 cup seasoned bread crumbs
- 1 medium onion, chopped
- 2 cloves garlic, chopped
- 2 eggs, beaten
- 2 tablespoons Worcestershire sauce
- 1 tablespoon Italian seasoning mix
- Kosher salt and ground black pepper, to season
- Glaze:
- 1/2 cup ketchup
- 1 tablespoon Dijon mustard
- 1/4 cup brown sugar

Directions:
1. Thoroughly combine all the ingredients for the meatloaf; press the meatloaf into a lightly greased baking pan.
2. Select the "Air Fry" function and adjust the temperature to 360 degrees F. Press the "Start" key.
3. When the display indicates "Add Food", add the baking pan to the cooking tray. Air fry the pork meatloaf for 35 minutes.
4. Mix the glaze ingredients and spread them over the top of your meatloaf.
5. Select the "Broil" function and cook the meatloaf for 5 minutes more. Bon appétit!

Nutrition:
- Info398 Calories,23.3g Fat,18.3g Carbs,28g Protei.

Pork Shoulder With Sweet Potatoes

Servings: 5
Cooking Time: 1 Hour
Ingredients:

- 2 pounds pork shoulder
- 2 tablespoons olive oil
- 1 pound sweet potatoes, peeled
- Sea salt and ground black pepper, to taste

Directions:

1. Select the "Air Fry" function and adjust the temperature to 360 degrees F. Press the "Start" key. Place aluminum foil onto the drip pan.
2. Toss the pork shoulder with olive oil.
3. When the display indicates "Add Food", place the pork in the air fryer oven perforated pan. Reserve the marinade. Cook the pork for about 30 minutes.
4. Toss the sweet potatoes with the remaining 1 tablespoon of olive oil, salt, and black pepper and add them to the air fryer oven perforated pan.
5. Baste the pork with the reserved marinade and continue to roast for 30 minutes more or until cooked through. Serve warm and enjoy!

Nutrition:

- Info450 Calories,28g Fat,16.8g Carbs,33.6g Protei.

Easy Scotch Fillets

Servings: 4
Cooking Time: 20 Minutes + Marinating Time
Ingredients:

- 1 ½ pounds Scotch fillet
- 2 tablespoons butter, softened
- 2 cloves garlic, minced
- 1 tablespoon Dijon mustard
- 2 tablespoons fresh parsley, chopped
- 1/2 teaspoon cumin seeds
- 1 teaspoon cayenne pepper
- Kosher salt and freshly ground black pepper, to taste

Directions:

1. Add all the ingredients to a ceramic or glass bowl. Allow the beef to marinate for at least 3 hours.
2. Select the "Air Fry" function and adjust the temperature to 365 degrees F. Press the "Start" key. Place aluminum foil onto the drip pan.
3. When the display indicates "Add Food", place the beef in the air fryer oven perforated pan. Reserve the marinade. Cook the beef for about 12 minutes.

4. Increase the temperature of the oven to 400 degrees F; baste the beef with the reserved marinade and continue to cook for 5 to 6 minutes more.
5. Serve warm and enjoy!
Nutrition:

- Info300 Calories,16g Fat,1.2g Carbs,35.6g Protei.

Beef Brisket With Brussels Sprouts

Servings: 5
Cooking Time: 50 Minutes
Ingredients:

- 1 ½ pounds beef brisket
- 1 pound Brussels sprouts
- 2 garlic cloves, minced
- 1 teaspoon paprika
- Sea salt and ground black pepper, to taste
- 1/2 teaspoon ground cumin
- 1 teaspoon stone-ground mustard
- 2 tablespoons butter
- 1 cup barbecue sauce
- 1 tablespoon Worcestershire sauce

Directions:

1. Select the "Air Fry" function and adjust the temperature to 350 degrees F. Press the "Start" key.
2. Toss the beef and Brussels sprouts with the other ingredients. Place aluminum foil onto the drip pan.
3. When the display indicates "Add Food", place the beef in the air fryer oven perforated pan. Cook the beef for about 35 minutes.
4. Turn the temperature to 390 degrees F. Turn them over, add in the Brussels sprouts, and continue to cook for 15 minutes longer.
5. Serve warm and enjoy!
Nutrition:

- Info461 Calories,25.7g Fat,34g Carbs,24.2g Protei.

Mom's Herbed Meatballs

Servings: 4
Cooking Time: 20 Minutes
Ingredients:

- 1 pound ground beef
- 3 green onions, chopped
- 2 green garlic stalks, chopped (or garlic cloves)
- 1/4 cup fresh parsley, chopped
- 2 tablespoons fresh basil, chopped
- 1 tablespoon fresh coriander, chopped
- 1 teaspoon Montreal seasoning mix
- 2 eggs lightly beaten
- 1/2 cup seasoned breadcrumbs
- 1 tablespoon Worcestershire sauce
- 1 teaspoon cayenne pepper
- Kosher salt and ground black pepper, to taste

Directions:

1. Select the "Air Fry" function and adjust the temperature to 390 degrees F. Press the "Start" key.
2. Place a sheet of parchment paper in the air fryer oven pan. Thoroughly combine all the ingredients in a mixing bowl.
3. Form the mixture into eight balls and place them in a single layer in the air fryer oven perforated pan.
4. Air fry the meatballs for 18 minutes or until they reach an internal temperature of 165 degrees F on a meat thermometer. Bon appétit!

Nutrition:

- Info327 Calories,16.9g Fat,14.4g Carbs,26.3g Protei.

Entrecôte Steak With Cauliflower

Servings: 4
Cooking Time: 20 Minutes
Ingredients:

- 1 ½ pounds Entrecôte steaks
- Salt and ground black pepper, to taste
- 1 tablespoon Dijon mustard
- 1 tablespoon olive oil
- 1 pound cauliflower florets

Directions:

1. Toss the steaks with salt, black pepper, mustard, and olive oil.
2. Select the "Air Fry" function and adjust the temperature to 380 degrees F. Press the "Start" key. Place aluminum foil onto the drip pan.
3. When the display indicates "Add Food", place the beef in the air fryer oven perforated pan. Reserve the marinade. Cook the beef for about 5 minutes.
4. Add in the cauliflower florets. Increase the temperature of the oven to 400 degrees F and continue to cook for 12 minutes more.
5. Serve warm and enjoy!

Nutrition:

- Info450 Calories,30.2g Fat,6.9g Carbs,37.6g Protei.

Thai-style Beef Roast

Servings: 5
Cooking Time: 50 Minutes
Ingredients:

- 2 pounds beef tenderloin roast
- 2 tablespoons olive oil
- 2 garlic cloves, minced
- 2 tablespoons soy sauce
- 2 tablespoons Thai sweet chili sauce
- 2 rosemary sprigs, chopped
- 1 thyme sprig, chopped
- 1 teaspoon red pepper flakes, crushed
- Coarse sea salt and ground black pepper, to taste

Directions:

1. Select the "Roast" function and adjust the temperature to 360 degrees F. Set the oven to "Rotate" and set the time to 45 minutes. Press the "Start" key.
2. Pat the beef dry. Rub the olive oil, garlic, soy sauce, Thai sauce, and spices all over the round roast.
3. When the display indicates "Add Food", place the beef in the rotisserie basket.
4. Roast the beef until it reaches an internal temperature of 160 degrees F on a meat thermometer.
5. Bon appétit!

Nutrition:

- Info433 Calories,23.9g Fat,4.1g Carbs,50g Protei.

Smoked Sausage With Cauliflower

Servings: 5
Cooking Time: 15 Minutes
Ingredients:

- 1 pound smoked sausages
- 1 pound cauliflower florets
- 2 tablespoons soy sauce
- 1 teaspoon Italian seasoning blend
- Sea salt and ground black pepper, to taste

Directions:

1. Select the "Air Fry" function and adjust the temperature to 400 degrees F. Press the "Start" key. Place aluminum foil onto the drip pan.
2. Toss all the ingredients in a mixing bowl.
3. When the display indicates "Add Food", place the sausage and cauliflower in the air fryer oven perforated pan. Cook the sausage and cauliflower for about 5 minutes.
4. Turn them over and continue to cook for a further 5 minutes.
5. Bon appétit!

Nutrition:

- Info369 Calories,26.2g Fat,11.1g Carbs,19.7g Protei.

Chinese-style Pork Meatballs

Servings: 4
Cooking Time: 20 Minutes
Ingredients:

- 1 pound ground pork
- 1 egg
- 1/2 cup crushed crackers
- 1 small onion, chopped
- 2 cloves garlic, minced
- 2 tablespoons cilantro, chopped
- 2 tablespoons parsley, chopped
- Sea salt and freshly ground black pepper, to taste
- Five-spice powder (optional)
- 2 tablespoons soy sauce
- 2 tablespoons tomato sauce
- A dash of Tabasco sauce

Directions:

1. Select the "Air Fry" function and adjust the temperature to 380 degrees F. Press the "Start" key.
2. Place a sheet of parchment paper in the air fryer oven pan.

3. In a mixing bowl, thoroughly combine all the ingredients. Then, drop rounds of the mixture in a single layer onto the prepared pan using a small scoop.
4. Air fry the meatballs for 10 minutes.
5. Select the "Broil" function and cook your meatballs for a further 5 minutes or until cooked through.
6. Bon appétit!

Nutrition:

- Info397 Calories,28.2g Fat,12.5g Carbs,22.8g Protei.

Top Round Steak

Servings: 4
Cooking Time: 20 Minutes + Marinating Time
Ingredients:

- 1 ½ pounds top round steak, cut into bite-sized cubes
- 2 tablespoons olive oil
- 1 tablespoon Italian seasoning
- 1 teaspoon cayenne pepper
- Sea salt and ground black pepper, to taste
- 1/4 cup butter
- 2 garlic cloves, minced
- 1 teaspoon fresh rosemary
- 1 teaspoon fresh thyme

Directions:

1. Add all the ingredients to a ceramic or glass bowl. Allow the beef to marinate for at least 3 hours.
2. Select the "Air Fry" function and adjust the temperature to 365 degrees F. Press the "Start" key. Place aluminum foil onto the drip pan.
3. When the display indicates "Add Food", place the beef in the air fryer oven perforated pan. Reserve the marinade. Cook the beef for about 12 minutes.
4. Increase the temperature of the oven to 400 degrees F; baste the beef with the reserved marinade and continue to cook for 5 to 6 minutes more.
5. Serve warm and enjoy!

Nutrition:

- Info453 Calories,31.4g Fat,3.1g Carbs,38.3g Protei.

Honey Garlic Rib Chops

Servings: 4
Cooking Time: 20 Minutes
Ingredients:

- 1 ½ pounds rib chops
- Kosher salt and freshly ground black pepper, to taste
- 1 teaspoon sage, minced
- 1 teaspoon basil, minced
- 1 teaspoon rosemary, minced
- 2 cloves garlic, minced
- 2 tablespoons olive oil
- 2 tablespoons honey

Directions:

1. Select the "Air Fry" function and adjust the temperature to 400 degrees F. Press the "Start" key. Now, grease the air fryer oven perforated pan with olive oil.
2. When the display indicates "Add Food", place the pork chops in the air fryer oven perforated pan.
3. Air fry them for 15 minutes or until the internal temperature reaches 145 degrees F on a meat thermometer.
4. Serve warm and enjoy!

Nutrition:

- Info419 Calories,25.5g Fat,9.1g Carbs,34.6g Protei.

Stuffed Beef Rolls

Servings: 4
Cooking Time: 25 Minutes + Marinating Time
Ingredients:

- 1 pound beef tenderloin, thinly sliced
- 2 tablespoons Worcestershire sauce
- 2 tablespoons yellow mustard
- 1 teaspoon dried oregano
- 1 teaspoon garlic powder
- 1 teaspoon onion powder
- 2 teaspoons olive oil
- 4 tablespoons mayonnaise
- 4 ounces Gruyere cheese, crumbled

Directions:

1. Place the beef, Worcestershire sauce, mustard, spices, and olive oil in a ceramic or glass bowl. Allow the beef to marinate for at least 3 hours.
2. Divide the mayonnaise and Gruyere cheese between the beef tenderloin slices; roll them up and secure with toothpicks.

3. Select the "Air Fry" function and adjust the temperature to 400 degrees F. Press the "Start" key. Place aluminum foil onto the drip pan.
4. When the display indicates "Add Food", place the beef in the air fryer oven perforated pan. Reserve the marinade.
5. Cook the beef rolls for about 20 minutes, basting them with the marinade occasionally.

Nutrition:

- Info482 Calories,37.1g Fat,3.9g Carbs,32g Protei.

Classic Pork Burgers

Servings: 4
Cooking Time: 20 Minutes
Ingredients:

- 1 pound ground pork
- 1 egg, whisked
- 1/2 cup bread crumbs
- 1/2 cup Parmesan cheese, grated
- 1 tablespoon dried parsley flakes
- Sea salt and ground black pepper, to taste
- 1 teaspoon cayenne pepper
- 4 hamburger buns, split
- 1 tablespoon Dijon mustard
- 4 large lettuce leaves
- 1 small onion, thinly sliced

Directions:

1. Thoroughly combine the ground pork, egg, bread crumbs, cheese, dried parsley, salt, black pepper, and cayenne pepper.
2. Shape the mixture into four patties.
3. Select the "Air Fry" function and adjust the temperature to 370 degrees F. Press the "Start" key. Place aluminum foil onto the drip pan.
4. When the display indicates "Add Food", place the pork burgers in the air fryer oven perforated pan. Cook your burgers for about 8 minutes.
5. Flip the burgers over and continue to cook them for a further 8 minutes. Arrange your burgers with hamburger buns, warm patties, mustard, lettuce, and onion.
6. Serve immediately and enjoy!

Nutrition:

- Info532 Calories,25.2g Fat,45.5g Carbs,35.6g Protei.

Asian-style Beef Bowl

Servings: 4
Cooking Time: 20 Minutes
Ingredients:
- 1 pound rib-eye steak, cubed
- 1/2 cup dashi (or beef bone stock)
- 4 tablespoons rice vinegar
- 2 tablespoons soy sauce (or Shoyu sauce)
- 1 teaspoon ginger-garlic paste
- 2 tablespoons agave nectar
- 1 teaspoon red pepper flakes, crushed
- Sea salt and ground black pepper, to taste
- 1 pound Chinese cabbage, cut into wedges
- 1 medium shallot, sliced

Directions:
1. Place the steak, dashi, rice vinegar, soy sauce, ginger-garlic paste, agave nectar, red pepper flakes, salt, and black pepper in a ceramic bowl. Cover and allow the beef to marinate for 3 hours.
2. Select the "Air Fry" function and adjust the temperature to 380 degrees F. Press the "Start" key. Place aluminum foil onto the drip pan.
3. When the display indicates "Add Food", place the steak, cabbage, and shallot in the parchment-lined air fryer oven perforated pan.
4. Cook the steak for about 8 minutes, turning it twice during the cooking time. Increase the temperature to 400 degrees F and continue cooking for 8 minutes more.
5. Serve warm and enjoy!

Nutrition:
- Info377 Calories,25.5g Fat,14.8g Carbs,23.3g Protei.

Asian-style Pork Butt

Servings: 5
Cooking Time: 50 Minutes + Marinating Time
Ingredients:
- 2 pounds pork butt
- 2 tablespoons agave syrup
- 2 tablespoons soy sauce
- 2 tablespoons Shaoxing wine
- 1 tablespoon fish sauce
- 2 garlic cloves, minced
- 1 teaspoon Five-spice powder

Directions:
1. Add all the ingredients to a ceramic or glass bowl. Allow the pork to marinate for at least 3 hours.

2. Select the "Air Fry" function and adjust the temperature to 390 degrees F. Press the "Start" key. Place aluminum foil onto the drip pan.
3. When the display indicates "Add Food", place the pork in the air fryer oven perforated pan. Reserve the marinade. Cook the pork for about 25 minutes.
4. Baste the pork with the reserved marinade and continue to roast for about 20 minutes or until cooked through. Serve warm and enjoy!

Nutrition:
- Info388 Calories,22.3g Fat,9.3g Carbs,34.4g Protei.

Hawaiian-style Pork Skewers

Servings: 4
Cooking Time: 30 Minutes
Ingredients:
- 1 pound pork loin, cut into bite-sized cubes
- 1/4 cup soy sauce
- 1/4 cup honey
- 1/4 cup olive oil
- 1 tablespoon chili sauce
- 4tablespoons apple cider vinegar
- 2 garlic cloves, minced
- 1 teaspoon crushed red pepper flakes
- 1 teaspoon ginger, peeled and grated
- Sea salt and ground black pepper, to taste
- 1 cup pineapple cubes
- 1 large onion, cut into wedges
- 2 bell peppers, sliced

Directions:
1. Toss all the ingredients in a ceramic bowl; let it marinate for 1 hour.
2. Select the "Roast" function and adjust the temperature to 360 degrees F. Press the "Start" key.
3. Lightly grease the air fryer oven perforated pan with olive oil.
4. Thread bamboo skewers, alternating with pork and veggies.
5. When the display indicates "Add Food", place the skewers in the air fryer oven perforated pan. Roast them for about 25 minutes, rotating them once or twice. Bon appétit!

Nutrition:
- Info458 Calories,21.1g Fat,39.5g Carbs,28.2g Protei.

Roast Pork With Crackling

Servings: 4
Cooking Time: 1 Hour
Ingredients:
- 1 ½ pounds pork butt, skin on
- 1 tablespoon olive oil
- Sea salt and ground black pepper, to taste
- 1 teaspoon smoked paprika
- 1 teaspoon mustard powder
- 1 teaspoon garlic powder

Directions:
1. Using the rotisserie spit, push through the pork butt and attach the rotisserie forks.
2. Select the "Roast" function and adjust the temperature to 380 degrees F. Set the oven to "Rotate" and set time to 50 minutes. Press the "Start" key.
3. When the display indicates "Add Food", place the prepared meat in the oven.
4. Select the "Broil" function and continue cooking for a further 5 minutes. Enjoy!

Nutrition:
- Info494 Calories,33.6g Fat,2.1g Carbs,43.1g Protei.

Sriracha Pork Burgers

Servings: 4
Cooking Time: 20 Minutes
Ingredients:
- 1 pound ground pork
- 1/2 cup instant oats
- 1 teaspoon dried basil
- 1 teaspoon dried oregano
- 1 medium onion, chopped
- 1 garlic clove, minced
- Sea salt and ground black pepper, to taste
- 4 hamburger buns
- 2 tablespoons sriracha

Directions:
1. Thoroughly combine the ground pork, instant oats, herbs, onion, garlic, salt, and black pepper.
2. Shape the mixture into four patties.
3. Select the "Air Fry" function and adjust the temperature to 370 degrees F. Press the "Start" key. Place aluminum foil onto the drip pan.
4. When the display indicates "Add Food", place the pork burgers in the air fryer oven perforated pan. Cook your burgers for about 8 minutes.
5. Flip the burgers over and continue to cook them for a further 8 minutes. Arrange your burgers with hamburger buns and sriracha sauce; add toppings of choice and enjoy!

Nutrition:
- Info430 Calories,29g Fat,27.3g Carbs,24.6g Protei.

Juicy Flat Beef Ribs

Servings: 4
Cooking Time: 20 Minutes + Marinating Time
Ingredients:
- 1 ½ pounds flat beef ribs
- 1 cup BBQ sauce
- 1 teaspoon smoked paprika
- 1/2 teaspoon chili powder
- 2 tablespoons brown sugar
- 1 teaspoon onion powder
- Kosher salt and ground black pepper, to taste

Directions:
1. Add all the ingredients to a ceramic or glass bowl. Allow the beef to marinate for at least 3 hours.
2. Select the "Air Fry" function and adjust the temperature to 360 degrees F. Press the "Start" key. Place aluminum foil onto the drip pan.
3. When the display indicates "Add Food", place the beef ribs in the air fryer oven perforated pan. Reserve the marinade. Cook the beef for about 15 minutes.
4. Serve immediately and enjoy!

Nutrition:
- Info472 Calories,33.2g Fat,11.5g Carbs,33.2g Protei.

Roasted Boston Butt

Servings: 6
Cooking Time: 45 Minutes
Ingredients:
- 2 pounds Boston butt
- 1 tablespoon Dijon mustard
- 1 teaspoon ancho chile powder
- 2 tablespoons white vinegar
- Sea salt and ground black pepper, to taste
- 1 tablespoon smoked paprika
- 1/2 teaspoon ground cumin
- 1/2 teaspoon dried oregano
- 2 tablespoons brown sugar

Directions:
1. Add all the ingredients to a ceramic or glass bowl. Allow the pork to marinate for at least 3 hours.
2. Select the "Air Fry" function and adjust the temperature to 390 degrees F. Press the "Start" key. Place aluminum foil onto the drip pan.
3. When the display indicates "Add Food", place the pork in the air fryer oven perforated pan. Reserve the marinade. Cook the pork for about 25 minutes.
4. Baste the pork with the reserved marinade and continue to roast for about 20 minutes or until cooked through. Serve warm and enjoy!

Nutrition:
- Info362 Calories,22.7g Fat,5.3g Carbs,32.1g Protei.

Bacon And Cheese Meatloaf

Servings: 6
Cooking Time: 25 Minutes
Ingredients:
- 1 pound ground chuck
- 1/3 pound bacon bits
- 1 large sweet onion, chopped
- 3 cloves garlic, minced
- 1 cup instant oats
- 1 tablespoon fresh parsley, minced
- Sea salt and ground black pepper, to taste
- 2 eggs, whisked
- 1 cup cream cheese, room temperature

Directions:
1. Thoroughly combine all the ingredients for the meatloaf; press the meatloaf into a lightly greased baking pan.
2. Select the "Air Fry" function and adjust the temperature to 400 degrees F. Press the "Start" key.
3. When the display indicates "Add Food", add the baking pan to the cooking tray. Air fry the meatloaf for 22 minutes.
4. Bon appétit!

Nutrition:
- Info512 Calories,35.1g Fat,24.5g Carbs,26.6g Protei.

Maple-glazed Pork Medallions

Servings: 4
Cooking Time: 20 Minutes
Ingredients:
- 1 pound pork medallions
- 1 teaspoon Dijon mustard
- 1/4 cup maple syrup
- 2 tablespoons balsamic vinegar
- 2 teaspoons olive oil
- 1 teaspoon cayenne pepper
- 1 teaspoon garlic powder
- 1 teaspoon onion powder
- Sea salt and freshly ground black pepper, to taste

Directions:
1. Select the "Air Fry" function and adjust the temperature to 400 degrees F. Press the "Start" key. Now, brush the air fryer oven perforated pan with nonstick oil.
2. Toss the pork medallions with the other ingredients.
3. When the display indicates "Add Food", place the pork medallions in the air fryer oven perforated pan.
4. Air fry them for 15 minutes or until the internal temperature reaches 145 degrees F on a meat thermometer.
5. Serve warm and enjoy!

Nutrition:
- Info297 Calories,14.9g Fat,15.5g Carbs,23.3g Protei.

Herbed Center Rib Chops

Servings: 5
Cooking Time: 20 Minutes
Ingredients:
- 2 pounds pork center rib chops
- 1 tablespoon butter
- 1 teaspoon dried oregano
- 1 teaspoon dried sage
- 1 teaspoon dried thyme
- 1 teaspoon dried paprika
- 1 teaspoon mustard powder
- 1 teaspoon garlic powder
- Kosher salt and ground black pepper, to taste

Directions:
1. Select the "Air Fry" function and adjust the temperature to 400 degrees F. Press the "Start" key. Now, grease the air fryer oven perforated pan with olive oil.
2. When the display indicates "Add Food", place the pork chops in the air fryer oven perforated pan.
3. Air fry them for 15 minutes or until the internal temperature reaches 145 degrees F on a meat thermometer.
4. Serve warm and enjoy!

Nutrition:
- Info289 Calories,11.2g Fat,1.8g Carbs,39.1g Protei.

Classic Porterhouse Steaks

Servings: 4
Cooking Time: 20 Minutes + Marinating Time
Ingredients:
- 1 ½ pounds Porterhouse steaks, cut into bite-sized chunks
- 1 teaspoon Montreal seasoning mix
- 2 tablespoons olive oil
- 2 garlic cloves, minced
- Sea salt and ground black pepper, to taste

Directions:
1. Add all the ingredients to a ceramic or glass bowl. Allow the beef to marinate for at least 3 hours.
2. Select the "Air Fry" function and adjust the temperature to 390 degrees F. Press the "Start" key. Place aluminum foil onto the drip pan.
3. When the display indicates "Add Food", place the beef in the air fryer oven perforated pan. Cook Porterhouse steaks for about 15 minutes.
4. Serve warm and enjoy!

Nutrition:
- Info418 Calories,29.3g Fat,0.9g Carbs,35.2g Protei.

Festive Pork Butt

Servings: 5
Cooking Time: 35 Minutes + Marinating Time
Ingredients:

- 2 pounds boneless pork butt
- 2 tablespoons olive oil
- 2 tablespoons red wine vinegar
- 1 tablespoon Dijon mustard
- 1 teaspoon cumin seeds
- 1 teaspoon fennel seeds
- 1 teaspoon cayenne pepper
- Kosher salt and ground black pepper, to taste
- 2 tablespoons brown sugar

Directions:

1. Add all the ingredients to a ceramic or glass bowl. Allow the pork to marinate for at least 3 hours.
2. Select the "Air Fry" function and adjust the temperature to 390 degrees F. Press the "Start" key. Place aluminum foil onto the drip pan.
3. When the display indicates "Add Food", place the pork in the air fryer oven perforated pan. Reserve the marinade. Cook the pork for about 15 minutes.
4. Baste the pork with the reserved marinade and continue to roast for about 15 minutes or until cooked through. Serve immediately and enjoy!

Nutrition:

- Info542 Calories,37.5g Fat,3.1g Carbs,45.4g Protei.

Smoked Paprika Meatballs

Servings: 4
Cooking Time: 20 Minutes
Ingredients:

- 1 ½ pounds ground pork
- 2 tablespoons butter
- Sea salt and ground black pepper, to taste
- 1 small onion, chopped
- 2 garlic cloves, minced
- 1 teaspoon mustard seeds
- 1 teaspoon smoked paprika
- 1/2 teaspoon ground cumin

Directions:

1. Select the "Air Fry" function and adjust the temperature to 380 degrees F. Press the "Start" key.
2. Place a sheet of parchment paper in the air fryer oven pan.
3. In a mixing bowl, thoroughly combine all the ingredients. Then, drop rounds of the mixture in a single layer onto the prepared pan using a small scoop.
4. Air fry the meatballs for 10 minutes.

5. Select the "Broil" function and cook your meatballs for a further 5 minutes or until cooked through.
6. Bon appétit!

Nutrition:

- Info511 Calories,42.1g Fat,3.8g Carbs,29g Protei.

Authentic Albondigas Mexicanas

Servings: 4
Cooking Time: 25 Minutes
Ingredients:

- 1 pound ground chuck
- 1 small leek, chopped
- 2 garlic cloves, minced
- 1 bell pepper, chopped
- 1 jalapeno pepper, chopped
- 2 large eggs, beaten
- 2 tablespoons olive oil
- 2 tablespoons fresh parsley, chopped
- 1 teaspoon Mexican oregano
- 1 bread slice, crustless and soaked in 2 tablespoons of milk
- 1/2 cup tortilla chips, crushed

Directions:

1. Select the "Air Fry" function and adjust the temperature to 390 degrees F. Press the "Start" key.
2. Place a sheet of parchment paper in the air fryer oven pan.
3. Thoroughly combine all the ingredients in a mixing bowl.
4. Form the mixture into 8 balls and place them in a single layer in the air fryer oven perforated pan, press each ball slightly using a fork.
5. Air fry the meatballs for 20 minutes. Bon appétit!

Nutrition:

- Info317 Calories,18.5g Fat,10.8g Carbs,27.1g Protei.

Breaded Filet Mignon

Servings: 5
Cooking Time: 15 Minutes
Ingredients:
- 1 ½ pounds filet mignon
- 1 medium egg
- 1 cup bread crumbs
- 1 tablespoon olive oil
- 1 teaspoon garlic powder
- 1 teaspoon onion powder
- 1 teaspoon mustard powder
- 1 teaspoon cayenne pepper
- Sea salt and ground black pepper, to taste

Directions:
1. Select the "Roast" function and adjust the temperature to 365 degrees F. Press the "Start" key.
2. Whisk the egg in a shallow bowl; in another shallow bowl, mix the remaining ingredients.
3. Dip the filet mignon into the whisked egg. Roll it into the crumb mixture.
4. When the display indicates "Add Food", place the beef in the air fryer oven perforated pan. Cook the beef for about 12 minutes.
5. Serve warm and enjoy!

Nutrition:
- Info255 Calories,10.2g Fat,5.5g Carbs,32.9g Protei.

Perfect Short Ribs

Servings: 4
Cooking Time: 20 Minutes + Marinating Time
Ingredients:
- 1 ½ pounds chuck short ribs
- 1/4 cup soy sauce
- 1/2 cup red wine
- 2 tablespoons olive oil
- 1/4 cup molasses
- 2 cloves garlic, pressed
- 1 teaspoon mustard seeds
- 1 teaspoon turmeric powder

Directions:
1. Add all the ingredients to a ceramic or glass bowl. Allow the beef to marinate for at least 3 hours.
2. Select the "Air Fry" function and adjust the temperature to 360 degrees F. Press the "Start" key. Place aluminum foil onto the drip pan.
3. When the display indicates "Add Food", place the beef ribs in the air fryer oven perforated pan. Reserve the marinade. Cook the beef for about 15 minutes.
4. Serve immediately and enjoy!

Nutrition:
- Info453 Calories,25.1g Fat,21.2g Carbs,35.8g Protei.

Pork Chops With Cauliflower

Servings: 4
Cooking Time: 20 Minutes
Ingredients:
- 1 ½ pounds boneless pork chops
- 1 teaspoon brown mustard
- 1 tablespoon butter
- 1/2 cup seasoned breadcrumbs
- Coarse sea salt and ground black pepper, to taste
- 1 pound cauliflower florets

Directions:
1. Select the "Air Fry" function and adjust the temperature to 400 degrees F. Press the "Start" key. Now, grease the air fryer oven perforated pan with olive oil.
2. Toss the pork chops with mustard, butter, breadcrumbs, sea salt, and black pepper.
3. When the display indicates "Add Food", place the pork chops and cauliflower florets in the air fryer oven perforated pan.
4. Air fry them for 15 minutes or until cooked through. Bon appétit!

Nutrition:
- Info379 Calories,15.1g Fat,16.6g Carbs,40g Protei.

Crispy Pork Tenderloin

Servings: 4
Cooking Time: 25 Minutes
Ingredients:
- 1 ½ pounds pork tenderloin
- 2 large eggs
- 1/2 cup all-purpose flour
- 1 teaspoon paprika
- Kosher salt and freshly ground black pepper, to taste
- 1 cup tortilla chips, crushed
- 2 tablespoons butter, melted

Directions:
1. Select the "Air Fry" function and adjust the temperature to 400 degrees F. Press the "Start" key. Now, brush the air fryer oven perforated pan with nonstick oil.
2. Mix the eggs, flour, and spices in a shallow bowl. In another shallow bowl, mix the tortilla chips and butter.
3. Coat the pork chops with the flour mixture; then, coat the pork chops with the tortilla chips mixture.
4. When the display indicates "Add Food", place the pork chops in the air fryer oven perforated pan.
5. Air fry them for 20 minutes or until the internal temperature reaches 145 degrees F on a meat thermometer.
6. Serve warm and enjoy!

Nutrition:
- Info455 Calories,23.2g Fat,18.6g Carbs,40.5g Protei.

Sticky Chinese-style Pork

Servings: 4
Cooking Time: 40 Minutes + Marinating Time
Ingredients:
- 1 ½ pounds boneless pork butt
- 2 tablespoons cilantro, chopped
- 1/2 cup orange juice
- 1/4 cup sweet chili sauce
- 4 garlic cloves (finely chopped)
- 2 tablespoons sesame oil (or melted ghee)
- 1 teaspoon Chinese five-spice
- Kosher salt and ground black pepper, to taste

Directions:
1. Add all the ingredients to a ceramic or glass bowl. Allow the pork to marinate for at least 3 hours.
2. Select the "Air Fry" function and adjust the temperature to 390 degrees F. Press the "Start" key. Place aluminum foil onto the drip pan.
3. When the display indicates "Add Food", place the pork in the air fryer oven perforated pan. Reserve the marinade. Cook the pork for about 20 minutes.
4. Baste the pork with the reserved marinade and continue to roast for about 20 minutes or until cooked through. Serve immediately and enjoy!

Nutrition:
- Info418 Calories,27.9g Fat,8.1 Carbs,30.4g Protei.

Dijon Pork Chops

Servings: 4
Cooking Time: 20 Minutes
Ingredients:
- 1 ½ pounds pork blade chops
- 4 tablespoons mayonnaise
- 1 tablespoon Dijon mustard
- 1/2 cup seasoned breadcrumbs
- 1 teaspoon garlic powder
- 1/2 onion powder
- Sea salt and ground black pepper, to taste

Directions:
1. Select the "Air Fry" function and adjust the temperature to 400 degrees F. Press the "Start" key. Now, grease the air fryer oven perforated pan with olive oil.
2. Toss the pork chops with the other ingredients.
3. When the display indicates "Add Food", place the pork chops in the air fryer oven perforated pan.
4. Air fry them for 15 minutes or until the internal temperature reaches 145 degrees F on a meat thermometer.
5. Serve warm and enjoy!

Nutrition:

- Info425 Calories,23.9g Fat,13.1g Carbs,40g Protei

Saucy Pork Belly

Servings: 4
Cooking Time: 15 Minutes
Ingredients:
- 1 pound pork belly sliced, patted dry
- 1 tablespoon Worcestershire sauce
- 2 garlic cloves, pressed
- 1 teaspoon onion powder
- 1 teaspoon cayenne pepper
- Sea salt and ground black pepper, to taste
- 1/4 cup tomato sauce

Directions:
1. Add all the ingredients to a ceramic or glass bowl. Allow the pork to marinate for at least 30 minutes.
2. Select the "Air Fry" function and adjust the temperature to 350 degrees F. Press the "Start" key. Place aluminum foil onto the drip pan.
3. When the display indicates "Add Food", place the pork in the air fryer oven perforated pan. Cook the pork for about 5 minutes. Turn it over and continue to cook for a further 7 minutes.
4. Serve immediately and enjoy!

Nutrition:
- Info619 Calories,60.2g Fat,6.5g Carbs,11.5g Protei.

Summer-style Spareribs

Servings: 4
Cooking Time: 45 Minutes
Ingredients:
- 1 ½ pounds pork spareribs
- 2 tablespoons brown mustard
- 1 teaspoon cayenne pepper
- 1/2 teaspoon dried thyme
- 2 tablespoons Worcestershire sauce
- 1 teaspoon liquid smoke
- 1/4 cup apple cider vinegar
- 1/4 cup seedless blackberry preserves
- 1/2 cup cream of celery soup

Directions:
1. Place all the ingredients in a ceramic dish. Cover and let it marinate for at least 1 hour. Place aluminum foil onto the drip pan.
2. Select the "Air Fry" function and adjust the temperature to 350 degrees F. Press the "Start" key.
3. When the display indicates "Add Food", add the pork ribs to the rotisserie basket. Cook the pork ribs for about 40 minutes or until they are thoroughly cooked.
4. Bon appétit!

Nutrition:
- Info365 Calories,22.2g Fat,7.4g Carbs,33.5g Protei.

Rice, Grains And Pastry Recipes

Classic Baked Tortilla

Servings: 2
Cooking Time: 15 Minutes
Ingredients:
- 1 whole-wheat tortilla
- 2 tablespoons pizza sauce
- 1/4 cup Colby cheese, grated
- 1 tablespoon Kalamata olives, pitted and sliced
- 1 teaspoon dried oregano
- 1 teaspoon dried basil

Directions:
1. Select the "Air Fry" function and adjust the temperature to 390 degrees F. Press the "Start" key.
2. Spread your tortillas with pizza sauce.
3. Divide the cheese, olives, oregano, and basil among your tortillas. Place your tortillas on the air fryer tray that is previously greased with olive oil.
4. Bake your tortillas for 4 minutes. Flip them and bake for a further 4 minutes or until cooked through. Serve immediately!

Nutrition:
- Info288 Calories,15.4g Fat,23.9g Carbs,12.8g Protei.

Easy Greek Kolokythokeftéthes

Servings: 5
Cooking Time: 15 Minutes
Ingredients:
- 1 pound zucchini, grated
- 2 cups white rice, cooked and rinsed
- 1/2 cup plain flour
- 1 small red onion, chopped
- 2 garlic cloves, minced
- Sea salt and freshly ground black pepper, to season
- 2 tablespoons fresh dill weed, minced
- 2 tablespoons fresh parsley, minced
- 2 large egg, well-beaten
- 1 cup feta cheese, crumbled
- 2 tablespoons olive oil

Directions:
1. Select the "Air Fry" function and adjust the temperature to 400 degrees F. Press the "Start" key.
2. Place a sheet of parchment paper in the air fryer oven pan. Thoroughly combine all the ingredients.
3. Form the mixture into equal balls and place them in a single layer in the air fryer oven perforated pan.
4. Air fry the croquettes for 11 minutes or until golden brown. Serve hot and enjoy!

Nutrition:
- Info314 Calories,14.3g Fat,34g Carbs,12.7g Protei.

Mushroom And Oatmeal Fritters

Servings: 4
Cooking Time: 20 Minutes
Ingredients:
- 2 cups instant oats
- 1 cup cremini mushrooms, chopped
- 1 medium onion, finely chopped
- 2 garlic cloves, minced
- 2 tablespoons butter, room temperature
- 2 tablespoons marinara sauce
- 2 eggs, whisked

Directions:
1. Select the "Air Fry" function and adjust the temperature to 400 degrees F. Press the "Start" key.
2. Place a sheet of parchment paper in the air fryer oven pan. Thoroughly combine all the ingredients.
3. Form the mixture into equal patties and place them in a single layer in the air fryer oven perforated pan.
4. Air fry your fritters for 15 minutes or until golden brown.
5. Bon appétit!

Nutrition:
- Info407 Calories,13.3g Fat,56.3g Carbs,17.2g Protei.

Classic Tortilla Chips

Servings: 4
Cooking Time: 5 Minutes
Ingredients:
- 4 corn tortillas, cut into triangles
- 1 tablespoon olive oil
- Sea salt, to taste

Directions:
1. Select the "Air Fry" function and adjust the temperature to 390 degrees F. Press the "Start" key.
2. Toss your tortilla pieces with olive oil and salt.
3. Bake your chips for 3 minutes or until lightly browned; cook in batches.
4. Bon appétit!

Nutrition:
- Info168 Calories,6.2g Fat,24.1g Carbs,3.7g Protei.

Country-style Apple Oatmeal Fritters

Servings: 5
Cooking Time: 20 Minutes
Ingredients:

- 2 medium apples, peeled, cored and grated
- 1 cup instant oats
- 1/2 cup rice flour
- 1 teaspoon baking powder
- 1/2 teaspoon baking soda
- 1/2 cup brown sugar
- 2 medium eggs, whisked
- 2 tablespoons olive oil
- 1 teaspoon ground cinnamon
- A pinch of grated nutmeg
- A pinch of kosher salt

Directions:

1. Select the "Air Fry" function and adjust the temperature to 400 degrees F. Press the "Start" key.
2. Place a sheet of parchment paper in the air fryer oven pan. Thoroughly combine all the ingredients.
3. Air fry your fritters for 15 minutes or until golden brown and cooked through.
4. Bon appétit!

Nutrition:

- Info330 Calories,9.6g Fat,53.9g Carbs,8.7g Protei.

Old-fashioned Spelt Patties

Servings: 4
Cooking Time: 20 Minutes
Ingredients:

- 1 cup spelled flour
- 1 cup vegetable broth
- 1 onion, chopped
- 1 medium carrot, grated
- 1 celery stalk, grated
- 2 garlic cloves, minced
- 2 large eggs, whisked
- 1 teaspoon dried parsley flakes
- 1 teaspoon dried thyme
- 1 teaspoon dried oregano
- Sea salt and ground black pepper, to taste

Directions:

1. Select the "Air Fry" function and adjust the temperature to 400 degrees F. Press the "Start" key.
2. Place a sheet of parchment paper in the air fryer oven pan. Thoroughly combine all the ingredients.
3. Form the mixture into equal patties and place them in a single layer in the air fryer oven perforated pan.
4. Air fry the patties for 15 minutes or until golden brown. Serve hot and enjoy!

Nutrition:

- Info190 Calories,3.6g Fat,27.7g Carbs,9.1g Protei.

Authentic Italian Pizza

Servings: 2
Cooking Time: 15 Minutes
Ingredients:

- 2 packages of pizza dough
- 2 teaspoons extra-virgin olive oil
- 1/2 cup marinara sauce
- 1/2 teaspoon dried oregano
- 1 teaspoon dried basil
- Kosher salt and freshly ground black pepper, to taste
- 4 ounces mozzarella cheese, sliced

Directions:

1. Select the "Air Fry" function and adjust the temperature to 400 degrees F. Press the "Start" key.
2. Stretch the dough on a work surface. Spread the pizza crust with marinara sauce.
3. Top your pizza crust with the other ingredients. Place your pizza on the air fryer tray that is previously greased with olive oil.
4. Bake your pizza for 10 minutes. Serve warm and enjoy!

Nutrition:

- Info351 Calories,8.8g Fat,43.5g Carbs,24.7g Protei.

Homemade Pita Chips

Servings: 2
Cooking Time: 10 Minutes
Ingredients:

- 2 small pita bread pockets, cut into triangles
- 2 tablespoons extra-virgin olive oil
- Coarse sea salt and ground black pepper, to taste
- 1 teaspoon dried oregano

Directions:

1. Select the "Air Fry" function and adjust the temperature to 330 degrees F. Press the "Start" key.
2. Toss the pita triangles with olive oil and salt.
3. Bake your pita chips for 6 minutes or until lightly browned; toss the pita chips once or twice, working in batches.
4. Bon appétit!

Nutrition:

- Info207 Calories,13.9g Fat,18.2g Carbs,3.1g Protei.

Toasted Greek Pita

Servings: 2
Cooking Time: 10 Minutes
Ingredients:
- 2 large whole-wheat pitas
- 1/2 cup hummus
- 1 small onion, chopped
- 2 ounces feta cheese, crumbled
- 1 small tomato, sliced
- 2 tablespoons Kalamata olives, pitted and sliced
- Sea salt and ground black pepper, to season

Directions:
1. Assemble pita breads with the other ingredients; you can use a toothpick to secure your pitas.
2. Select the "Toast" function and press the "Start" key.
3. When the display indicates "Add Food", place the sandwich on the air fryer tray.
4. Toast the sandwich for about 3 minutes or so. Enjoy!

Nutrition:
- Info379 Calories,14g Fat,52.9g Carbs,13.8g Protei.

Chocolate Buckwheat Cakes

Servings: 4
Cooking Time: 20 Minutes
Ingredients:
- 1 cup buckwheat flour
- 1/2 cup plain flour
- 1 teaspoon baking powder
- 1 tablespoon brown sugar
- 2 tablespoons cocoa powder
- A pinch of kosher salt
- A pinch of grated nutmeg
- 2 medium eggs
- 1 cup plain milk
- 1 teaspoon pure vanilla extract
- 1 tablespoon butter, at room temperature

Directions:
1. In a mixing bowl, thoroughly combine the dry ingredients. In another bowl, whisk the wet ingredients. Add the wet mixture to the dry ingredients, and mix to combine well.
2. Grease a baking pan with nonstick cooking oil and set it aside.
3. Select the "Air Fry" function and adjust the temperature to 350 degrees F. Press the "Start" key.
4. Cook your pancakes for about 15 minutes, working in batches, if needed. Enjoy!

Nutrition:
- Info268 Calories,8.5g Fat,39.1g Carbs,10.6g Protei.

Wild Rice Patties

Servings: 4
Cooking Time: 15 Minutes
Ingredients:
- 2 cups cooked wild rice
- 1 cup plain flour
- 2 eggs, well-beaten
- 1 shallot, chopped
- 2 garlic cloves, minced
- Sea salt and ground black pepper, to taste
- 2 tablespoons olive oil

Directions:
1. Select the "Air Fry" function and adjust the temperature to 400 degrees F. Press the "Start" key.
2. Place a sheet of parchment paper in the air fryer oven pan. Thoroughly combine all the ingredients.
3. Form the mixture into equal patties and place them in a single layer in the air fryer oven perforated pan.
4. Air fry the patties for 11 minutes or until golden brown. Serve hot and enjoy!

Nutrition:
- Info295 Calories,9.4g Fat,43.3g Carbs,9.7g Protei.

Swiss Cheese Scones

Servings: 6
Cooking Time: 20 Minutes
Ingredients:
- 2 cups all-purpose flour
- 1 cup Swiss cheese, shredded
- 1 teaspoon baking powder
- 1 teaspoon baking soda
- 1 teaspoon honey
- 1/2 teaspoon salt
- A pinch of grated nutmeg
- 1/4 cup olive oil
- 2 eggs, beaten
- 3/4 cup milk

Directions:
1. In a mixing bowl, thoroughly combine all the dry ingredients. In another bowl, mix all the wet ingredients.
2. Add the wet mixture to the dry mixture; mix until everything is combined well.
3. Spoon the dough into a lightly greased muffin tin.
4. Select the "Air Fry" function and adjust the temperature to 380 degrees F. Press the "Start" key.
5. Air fry your scones for 20 minutes, checking them occasionally to make sure they are not getting too brown on top.
6. Bon appétit!

Nutrition:
- Info359 Calories,17.6g Fat,35.5g Carbs,13.1g Protei.

Herb Millet Patties

Servings: 4
Cooking Time: 20 Minutes
Ingredients:

- 1 ½ cups millet, cooked
- 1 teaspoon baking powder
- 2 eggs, beaten
- 1 medium onion, chopped
- 2 cloves garlic, pressed
- 2 teaspoons olive oil
- 1 teaspoon ground turmeric
- 1 teaspoon ground coriander
- 1 teaspoon ground cumin
- 1 teaspoon smoked paprika
- A pinch of grated nutmeg
- Sea salt and ground black pepper, to taste
- 2 tablespoons fresh basil, roughly chopped
- 2 tablespoons fresh parsley, roughly chopped
- 1 cup tortilla chips, crushed

Directions:
1. Select the "Air Fry" function and adjust the temperature to 390 degrees F. Press the "Start" key.
2. Brush a baking pan with olive oil and set it aside.
3. In a mixing bowl, thoroughly combine all the ingredients. Shape the mixture into equal patties and place them on the prepared baking pan.
4. Cook the patties for about 15 minutes, turning them over halfway through the cooking time. Bon appétit!

Nutrition:
- Info315 Calories,12.5g Fat,42.8g Carbs,8.2g Protei.

Greek Pita Wraps

Servings: 2
Cooking Time: 15 Minutes
Ingredients:

- 2 Greek-style pitas
- 1/2 cup bacon bits
- 1/4 cup hummus
- 1/4 cup tomato sauce
- 1 cup haloumi cheese, crumbled

Directions:
1. Select the "Air Fry" function and adjust the temperature to 390 degrees F. Press the "Start" key.
2. Assemble pita wraps with Greek pitas and the remaining ingredients. Secure your wraps with toothpicks.
3. Bake your wraps for 8 minutes or until lightly browned.
4. Serve immediately!

Nutrition:
- Info285 Calories,11.4g Fat,35.2g Carbs,12.7g Protei.

Spelt Burgers With Herbs

Servings: 4
Cooking Time: 20 Minutes
Ingredients:

- 2 cups hulled spelt, cooked
- 1 carrot, grated
- 2 tablespoons parsley, chopped
- 2 tablespoons cilantro, chopped
- 2 tablespoons scallions, chopped
- 1/2 cup goat cheese, grated
- 1 egg
- Sea salt and freshly ground pepper, to taste

Directions:
1. Select the "Air Fry" function and adjust the temperature to 400 degrees F. Press the "Start" key.
2. Place a sheet of parchment paper in the air fryer oven pan. Thoroughly combine all the ingredients.
3. Form the mixture into equal patties and place them in a single layer in the air fryer oven perforated pan.
4. Air fry the patties for 15 minutes or until golden brown. Serve hot and enjoy!

Nutrition:
- Info365 Calories,7.4g Fat,63g Carbs,17.8g Protei.

Middle Eastern Pita Sandwich

Servings: 2
Cooking Time: 10 Minutes
Ingredients:

- 2 large pitas
- 4 tablespoons hummus
- 1 medium tomato, sliced
- 1 small cucumber, sliced
- 1 teaspoon za'atar
- 2 teaspoons olive oil
- 4 tablespoons Greek-style yogurt
- 1 clove garlic, minced
- Sea salt and cayenne pepper, to taste

Directions:
1. Assemble the pita breads with the other ingredients; you can use a toothpick to secure your pitas.
2. Select the "Toast" function and press the "Start" key.
3. When the display indicates "Add Food", place the sandwich on the air fryer tray.
4. Toast the sandwich for about 4 minutes or so. Enjoy!

Nutrition:
- Info298 Calories,8.9g Fat,45.1g Carbs,10.9g Protei.

Easy Cinnamon Donuts

Servings: 8
Cooking Time: 15 Minutes
Ingredients:
- 1 can jumbo biscuits
- 4 teaspoons butter melted
- 1/2 cup granulated sugar
- 1 teaspoon ground cinnamon

Directions:
1. Select the "Air Fry" function and adjust the temperature to 375 degrees F. Press the "Start" key.
2. Spritz the air fryer oven perforated pan with cooking oil. Separate the dough into eight biscuits.
3. Bake in the preheated air fryer for 4 minutes. Flip the donuts and air fry for an additional 4 minutes.
4. Mix the butter, sugar, and cinnamon. Then, cover the donuts with the sugar mixture by dipping and rolling around.
5. Bon appétit!

Nutrition:
- Info156 Calories,4.9g Fat,25.8g Carbs,1.9g Protei.

Sorghum Kabocha Croquettes

Servings: 4
Cooking Time: 15 Minutes
Ingredients:
- 1 kabocha squash, diced
- 1 cup sorghum flour
- 1 cup breadcrumbs
- 1 medium onion, chopped
- 1 teaspoon sage
- 1/2 teaspoon cayenne pepper
- Sea salt and freshly cracked black pepper, to taste
- 2 cloves garlic, pressed
- 1/2 cup buttermilk
- 2 tablespoons olive oil

Directions:
1. Select the "Air Fry" function and adjust the temperature to 400 degrees F. Press the "Start" key.
2. Place a sheet of parchment paper in the air fryer oven pan. Thoroughly combine all the ingredients.
3. Form the mixture into equal balls and place them in a single layer in the air fryer oven perforated pan.
4. Air fry the balls for 13 minutes or until golden brown. Bon appétit!

Nutrition:
- Info237 Calories,8.6g Fat,36.2g Carbs,5.8g Protei.

Bulgur And Lentil Croquettes

Servings: 4
Cooking Time: 20 Minutes
Ingredients:
- 2 cups bulgur, cooked and rinsed
- 1 cup red lentils, cooked or boiled
- 1/2 cup breadcrumbs
- 1 medium red beet, shredded and diced
- 1 medium onion, roughly chopped
- 2 cloves garlic, minced
- Kosher salt and freshly ground black pepper, to taste
- 1 teaspoon cayenne pepper
- 1 teaspoon thyme, chopped
- 2 tablespoons tahini

Directions:
1. Select the "Air Fry" function and adjust the temperature to 400 degrees F. Press the "Start" key.
2. Place a sheet of parchment paper in the air fryer oven pan. Thoroughly combine all the ingredients.
3. Form the mixture into equal balls and place them in a single layer in the air fryer oven perforated pan.
4. Air fry the croquettes for 15 minutes or until cooked through. Serve hot and enjoy!

Nutrition:
- Info331 Calories,5.6g Fat,56.4g Carbs,16.7g Protei.

Mexican Roll-ups

Servings: 2
Cooking Time: 15 Minutes
Ingredients:
- 4 small flour tortillas
- 1/2 cup salsa sauce
- 4 ounces pork chorizo, chopped
- 1/2 cup Queso Blanco cheese, shredded
- 2 green onion stalks, sliced

Directions:
1. Select the "Air Fry" function and adjust the temperature to 390 degrees F. Press the "Start" key.
2. Assemble the roll-ups with tortillas and the remaining ingredients. Secure them with toothpicks.
3. Bake your roll-ups for 8 minutes or until lightly browned.
4. Bon appétit!

Nutrition:
- Info507 Calories,19.2g Fat,53.3g Carbs,29.2g Protei.

Mediterranean-style Calzone

Servings: 2
Cooking Time: 15 Minutes
Ingredients:
- 2 large lavash flatbread
- 2 teaspoon olive oil
- 1/4 cup marinara sauce
- 4 ounces parmesan cheese, grated
- 2 ounces black olives, pitted and sliced
- 1 teaspoon dried oregano
- 1 teaspoon dried basil

Directions:
1. Select the "Air Fry" function and adjust the temperature to 390 degrees F. Press the "Start" key.
2. Assemble the Mediterranean calzone with lavash and the remaining ingredients. Fold the lavash bread in half, and pat the edges so that it is tightly closed.
3. Bake your Mediterranean calzone for 8 minutes or until lightly browned.
4. Bon appétit!

Nutrition:
- Info518 Calories,30.6g Fat,35.5g Carbs,23.6g Protei.

Baked Two-cheese Tortilla

Servings: 2
Cooking Time: 15 Minutes
Ingredients:
- 2 flour tortillas
- 3 tablespoons pizza sauce
- 2 ounces cheddar cheese, sliced
- 2 ounces mozzarella cheese, sliced

Directions:
1. Select the "Air Fry" function and adjust the temperature to 380 degrees F. Press the "Start" key.
2. Spread your tortillas with pizza sauce.
3. Top the pizza crust with cheese. Place your tortillas on the air fryer tray that is previously greased with olive oil.
4. Bake your tortillas for 4 minutes. Flip your tortillas and air fry them for a further 4 minutes or until lightly browned.
5. Bon appétit!

Nutrition:
- Info345 Calories,17.5g Fat,27.3g Carbs,18.8g Protei.

Barley Griddle Cake

Servings: 4
Cooking Time: 20 Minutes
Ingredients:
- 1/2 cup barley flour
- 1/2 cup plain flour
- 1/4 cup instant oats
- 1 teaspoon baking powder
- 1 teaspoon granulated sugar
- A pinch of kosher salt
- 1 large egg
- 1 cup plain milk
- 2 tablespoons butter, melted

Directions:
1. In a mixing bowl, thoroughly combine the dry ingredients. In another bowl, whisk the wet ingredients. Add the wet mixture to the dry ingredients, and mix to combine well.
2. Grease a baking pan with nonstick cooking oil and set it aside.
3. Select the "Air Fry" function and adjust the temperature to 350 degrees F. Press the "Start" key.
4. Cook your cakes for about 15 minutes, working in batches, if needed. Enjoy!

Nutrition:
- Info277 Calories,10.1g Fat,37.7g Carbs,8.9g Protei.

Mexican-style Bulgur Patties

Servings: 4
Cooking Time: 20 Minutes
Ingredients:
- 2 cups bulgur wheat
- 2 tablespoons olive oil
- 1 tablespoon tomato paste
- 1 teaspoon Mexican oregano
- 1 teaspoon ancho chili powder
- 1 teaspoon cayenne pepper
- Kosher salt and ground black pepper, to taste
- 1 teaspoon lime zest
- 1 medium onion, chopped
- 2 garlic cloves, minced
- 1 cup canned or boiled pinto beans, rinsed
- 1/2 cup Mexican-blend cheese, shredded
- 1/2 cup tortilla chips, crushed

Directions:
1. Select the "Air Fry" function and adjust the temperature to 400 degrees F. Press the "Start" key.
2. Place a sheet of parchment paper in the air fryer oven pan. Thoroughly combine all the ingredients.
3. Form the mixture into equal patties and place them in a single layer in the air fryer oven perforated pan.
4. Air fry the patties for 15 minutes or until cooked through. Serve hot and enjoy!

Nutrition:
- Info353 Calories,15.1g Fat,45g Carbs,11.9g Protei.

Spicy Oatmeal Patties

Servings: 4
Cooking Time: 20 Minutes
Ingredients:

- 1 ½ cups rolled oats
- 1/2 cup plain flour
- 2 tablespoons olive oil, divided
- 1 medium onion, chopped
- 2 garlic cloves, minced
- 2 eggs, beaten
- 1 teaspoon red pepper flakes, crushed
- 1 teaspoon ground coriander
- 2 tablespoons parsley, chopped
- 2 tablespoons cilantro, chopped
- 2 tablespoons chives, chopped
- 1 cup Cheddar cheese, shredded
- Sea salt and ground black pepper, to taste

Directions:

1. Select the "Air Fry" function and adjust the temperature to 400 degrees F. Press the "Start" key.
2. Place a sheet of parchment paper in the air fryer oven pan. Thoroughly combine all the ingredients.
3. Form the mixture into equal patties and place them in a single layer in the air fryer oven perforated pan.
4. Air fry the patties for 15 minutes or until golden brown. Serve hot and enjoy!

Nutrition:

- Info500 Calories,22.4g Fat,55.3g Carbs,21.7g Protei.

Easy Breakfast Granola

Servings: 10
Cooking Time: 45 Minutes
Ingredients:

- 1 ½ cups rolled oats
- 1 cup walnuts
- 1/2 cup pine nuts
- 1/2 cup pumpkin seeds, hulled
- 1/2 cup sunflower seeds, hulled
- 1/4 cup maple syrup
- 2 tablespoons coconut oil
- 1 teaspoon cinnamon
- 1/2 teaspoon ground cinnamon
- A pinch of sea salt
- A pinch of grated nutmeg
- 1/2 cup flaked coconut

Directions:

1. Select the "Air Fry" function and adjust the temperature to 260 degrees F. Press the "Start" key.
2. Line the air fryer tray with a piece of parchment paper.
3. Thoroughly combine all ingredients and spread the mixture onto the parchment-lined air fryer tray.
4. Bake your granola for 40 minutes, rotating the pan once or twice during cooking.
5. This granola can be kept in an airtight container for up to 2 weeks. Bon appétit!

Nutrition:

- Info323 Calories,22g Fat,26g Carbs,9.7g Protei.

Barley Vegetable Fritters

Servings: 4
Cooking Time: 20 Minutes
Ingredients:

- 2 cups barley, cooked
- 1 medium stalk celery, chopped
- 1 medium carrot, finely chopped
- 2 garlic cloves, minced
- 2 scallion stalks, chopped
- Sea salt and ground black pepper, to taste
- 1 teaspoon dried parsley
- 1 teaspoon dried oregano
- 1 teaspoon dried basil
- 1 cup seasoned breadcrumbs
- 2 tablespoons olive oil

Directions:

1. Select the "Air Fry" function and adjust the temperature to 400 degrees F. Press the "Start" key.
2. Place a sheet of parchment paper in the air fryer oven pan. Thoroughly combine all the ingredients.
3. Form the mixture into equal balls and place them in a single layer in the air fryer oven perforated pan.
4. Air fry the fritters for 15 minutes or until golden brown. Serve hot and enjoy!

Nutrition:

- Info218 Calories,7.7g Fat,34.1g Carbs,5.2g Protei.

Tejeringos With Spicy Chocolate

Servings: 4

Cooking Time: 15 Minutes

Ingredients:

- 1 can refrigerated biscuits
- 1/2 cup milk chocolate
- 1/2 teaspoon ground cayenne powder
- 1/2 cup pecans, coarsely chopped

Directions:

1. Select the "Air Fry" function and adjust the temperature to 375 degrees F. Press the "Start" key.
2. Spritz the air fryer oven perforated pan with cooking oil. Separate the dough into eight biscuits.
3. Bake in the preheated air fryer for 4 minutes. Flip the donuts and air fry for an additional 4 minutes.
4. Melt the chocolate in your microwave; whisk in the pepper and pecans. Then, cover the donuts with the chocolate mixture by dipping and rolling around.
5. Bon appétit!

Nutrition:

- Info327 Calories,21.8g Fat,32.4g Carbs,10.2g Protei.

Greek-style Pastry

Servings: 6

Cooking Time: 25 Minutes

Ingredients:

- 2 cups flour
- 1 teaspoon baking powder
- 1/2 teaspoon baking soda
- 1/2 kosher salt
- 1/2 cup Greek yogurt
- 1 large egg
- 1/4 cup honey
- 1/2 cup butter, at room temperature
- 2 ounces walnuts, coarsely chopped

Directions:

1. In a mixing bowl, thoroughly combine all the dry ingredients. In another bowl, mix all the wet ingredients.
2. Add the wet mixture to the dry mixture; fold in the walnuts and mix until everything is combined well.
3. Spoon the dough into a lightly greased muffin tin.
4. Select the "Air Fry" function and adjust the temperature to 380 degrees F. Press the "Start" key.
5. Air fry your scones for 20 minutes, checking them occasionally to make sure they are not getting too brown on top.
6. Bon appétit!

Nutrition:

- Info416 Calories,23.3g Fat,45.7g Carbs,7.7g Protei.

Italian-style Oatmeal Cheeseburgers

Servings: 4

Cooking Time: 20 Minutes

Ingredients:

- 2 cups quick-cooking oats
- 1 small onion, chopped
- 2 tablespoons olive oil
- 1/2 cup cheddar cheese, shredded
- 2 garlic cloves, minced
- 1 tablespoon Italian seasoning mix
- 1 teaspoon smoked paprika
- Sea salt and ground black pepper, to taste

Directions:

1. Select the "Air Fry" function and adjust the temperature to 400 degrees F. Press the "Start" key.
2. Place a sheet of parchment paper in the air fryer oven pan. Thoroughly combine all the ingredients.
3. Form the mixture into equal patties and place them in a single layer in the air fryer oven perforated pan.
4. Air fry the patties for 15 minutes or until golden brown. Serve hot and enjoy!

Nutrition:

- Info385 Calories,12.4g Fat,56.3g Carbs,13.7g Protei.

Desserts Recipes

Nutty Granola Bars

Servings: 7
Cooking Time: 35 Minutes
Ingredients:
- 1/2 cup almond meal
- 1 cup rolled oats
- 1/2 cup packed dates, pitted
- 1/2 cup raisins
- 1/4 cup honey
- 1/4 teaspoon coarse sea salt
- 1/2 teaspoon ground almonds
- 1/4 cup almond butter (or peanut butter)
- 1/2 cup walnuts, roughly chopped (or peanuts)
- 1 teaspoon vanilla extract

Directions:
1. Select the "Air Fry" function and adjust the temperature to 360 degrees F. Press the "Start" key.
2. In a large mixing bowl, stir together all the dry ingredients. In another bowl, mix the wet ingredients.
3. Add the wet mixture to the dry ingredients and stir to combine well.
4. Press the batter onto a parchment-lined baking pan. Bake your bars for approximately 15 minutes or until golden brown.
5. Let it sit on a wire rack for 20 minutes before slicing and serving.
6. Bon appétit!

Nutrition:
- Info270 Calories,14.7g Fat,38.4g Carbs,5.4g Protei.

Classic Mini Cheesecakes

Servings: 8
Cooking Time: 25 Minutes
Ingredients:
- 1 ½ cups crackers, crushed
- 3 tablespoons honey
- 6 tablespoons coconut oil
- Filling:
- 24 ounces cream cheese, at room temperature
- 1 cup sugar
- 1 cup sour cream
- 4 large eggs, beaten
- 1 teaspoon vanilla extract
- A pinch of kosher salt
- A pinch of grated nutmeg

Directions:
1. Select the "Air Fry" function and adjust the temperature to 400 degrees F. Press the "Start" key.
2. Mix the crushed crackers, honey, and coconut oil; press the crust into silicone cupcake molds. Bake for 5 minutes and allow them to cool on wire racks.

3. Using an electric mixer, whip the cream cheese, sugar, and sour cream until fluffy; add one egg at a time and continue to beat until creamy. Finally, add the vanilla extract, salt, and grated nutmeg.
4. Pour the topping mixture on top of the crust. Bake the mini cheesecakes at 390 degrees F for 15 minutes.
5. Allow your mini cheesecakes to chill in the refrigerator before serving. Enjoy!

Nutrition:
- Info577 Calories,47.2g Fat,3.7g Carbs,9.8g Protei.

Fried Banana Slices

Servings: 1
Cooking Time: 20 Minutes
Ingredients:
- 1 large banana, peeled and sliced
- 1 tablespoon peanut oil
- 1 teaspoon ground cinnamon
- 1/2 teaspoon ground cardamom

Directions:
1. Select the "Air Fry" function and adjust the temperature to 350 degrees F. Press the "Start" key.
2. Toss the banana slices with the remaining ingredients. Bake the banana slices for 5 minutes. Then toss them and continue to cook for 3 minutes longer.
3. Bon appétit!

Nutrition:
- Info251 Calories,14g Fat,33.8g Carbs,1.7g Protei.

Baked Plums With Almond Topping

Servings: 4
Cooking Time: 15 Minutes
Ingredients:
- 8 fresh plums, pitted and halved
- 2 teaspoons coconut oil
- 8 teaspoons ground almonds
- 8 teaspoons coconut sugar

Directions:
1. Top the plum halves with the remaining ingredients.
2. Select the "Air Fry" function and adjust the temperature to 350 degrees F. Press the "Start" key.
3. Bake the plum halves for 10 minutes or until tender and lightly caramelized.
4. Serve at room temperature and enjoy!

Nutrition:
- Info136 Calories,5.6g Fat,21.3g Carbs,2.2g Protei.

Candied Honey Pecans

Servings: 8
Cooking Time: 15 Minutes
Ingredients:
- 1/2 pound pecan halves
- 1 egg white
- 1 tablespoon fresh orange juice
- 2 tablespoons brown sugar
- 1/2 cup honey
- 1 teaspoon ground cinnamon
- A pinch of grated nutmeg
- A pinch of coarse sea salt

Directions:
1. Select the "Roast" function and adjust the temperature to 320 degrees F. Press the "Start" key.
2. In a mixing dish, toss all the ingredients.
3. When the display indicates "Add Food", place the almonds in the air fryer oven pan.
4. Roast your pecans in the preheated air fryer for 8 minutes, tossing them halfway through the cooking time to ensure even cooking.
5. Bon appétit!

Nutrition:
- Info277 Calories,20.3g Fat,25g Carbs,3.2g Protei.

Father's Day Croissants

Servings: 4
Cooking Time: 20 Minutes
Ingredients:
- 1 can refrigerated crescent rolls
- 1/2 cup chocolate spread
- 1/4 cup raisins, soaked in dark rum
- 1/4 cup almonds, chopped
- 1 large egg, whisked

Directions:
1. Separate the crescent rolls into eight triangles. Spread each triangle with chocolate spread, raisins, and almonds. Roll them up and lower them into the baking pan.
2. Brush the whisked egg on top of each croissant.
3. Select the "Air Fry" function and adjust the temperature to 350 degrees F. Press the "Start" key.
4. Air fry your croissants at 340 degrees F for about 15 minutes or until golden brown.
5. Bon appétit!

Nutrition:
- Info437 Calories,34.3g Fat,22.5g Carbs,10.4g Protei.

Grandma's Baked Apples

Servings: 6
Cooking Time: 20 Minutes
Ingredients:
- 6 medium apples, cored and sliced
- 2 tablespoons fresh lemon juice
- 2 teaspoons coconut oil, melted
- 1/2 cup brown sugar
- 1/2 teaspoon ground cardamom
- 1/4 teaspoon grated nutmeg
- 1 teaspoon ground cinnamon
- 1/2 teaspoon ginger, peeled and minced
- 2 tablespoons cornstarch

Directions:
1. Grease a baking pan with nonstick oil and set it aside.
2. Toss all the ingredients in the prepared baking pan.
3. Select the "Air Fry" function and adjust the temperature to 350 degrees F. Press the "Start" key. When the display indicates "Add Food", place the baking pan on the air fryer tray.
4. Bake the apples for about 15 minutes. Pierce the apples with a fork to ensure they are tender.
5. Enjoy!

Nutrition:
- Info187 Calories,1.8g Fat,45.1g Carbs,0.5g Protei.

Cinnamon Candied Walnuts

Servings: 6
Cooking Time: 10 Minutes
Ingredients:
- 2 cups raw walnut halves
- 1/4 cup brown sugar
- 1/2 teaspoon coarse sea salt
- 1 teaspoon ground cinnamon
- 1 teaspoon vanilla extract
- 1 egg white, whisked

Directions:
1. Select the "Roast" function and adjust the temperature to 320 degrees F. Press the "Start" key.
2. In a mixing dish, toss all the ingredients.
3. When the display indicates "Add Food", place the almonds in the air fryer oven pan.
4. Roast your walnuts in the preheated air fryer for 8 minutes, tossing them halfway through the cooking time to ensure even cooking.
5. Bon appétit!

Nutrition:
- Info247 Calories,22g Fat,9.2g Carbs,5.7g Protei.

Carrot Cupcakes With Almonds

Servings: 6
Cooking Time: 20 Minutes
Ingredients:

- 1 cup self-raising flour
- 1/2 cup granulated sugar
- 2 tablespoons maple syrup
- 1 teaspoon ground cinnamon
- 1/2 teaspoon ground cardamom
- 1/4 teaspoon grated nutmeg
- 2 medium carrots, trimmed and grated
- 2 tablespoons almond milk
- 2 medium eggs, beaten
- 1 stick butter, melted
- 2 tablespoons almonds, chopped

Directions:

1. Brush a muffin tin with a nonstick cooking spray oil; set it aside.
2. Mix the dry ingredients, then, thoroughly combine the wet ingredients. Add the wet mixture to the dry mixture and mix until everything is well incorporated. Fold in the berries.
3. Select the "Bake" function and adjust the temperature to 330 degrees F. Press the "Start" key. When the display indicates "Add Food", place the muffin tin on the air fryer tray.
4. Bake the cupcakes for 15 minutes or until a tester comes out clean when inserted in the middle.
5. Bon appétit!

Nutrition:

- Info355 Calories,19.3g Fat,41.5g Carbs,5.4g Protei.

Easy Apple Crumble

Servings: 8
Cooking Time: 20 Minutes
Ingredients:

- 1/4 cup old-fashioned oats
- 1/4 cup coconut flour
- 1 teaspoon baking powder
- 1/2 cup brown sugar
- 1/4 cup coconut oil
- 1/2 teaspoon ground cinnamon
- 1/2 teaspoon ground allspice
- 1/4 teaspoon kosher salt
- Topping:
- 2 large apples, peeled, cored, and diced
- 2 teaspoons fresh lemon juice

- 4 tablespoons coconut oil
- 1 teaspoon vanilla extract
- 1/4 cup brown sugar

Directions:

1. Select the "Bake" function and adjust the temperature to 360 degrees F. Press the "Start" key.
2. Mix the oats, coconut flour, baking powder, sugar, coconut oil, cinnamon, allspice, and kosher salt. Mix until smooth and uniform.
3. Press the mixture into a lightly greased baking pan. Toss the apples with the remaining ingredients and place them on the crust.
4. Bake your crumble for approximately 12 minutes or until the topping is golden brown. Enjoy!

Nutrition:

- Info227 Calories,14.8g Fat,24.6g Carbs,1.5g Protei.

Greek-style Cheesecake

Servings: 10
Cooking Time: 25 Minutes
Ingredients:

- 1 cup cracker crumbs
- 1/2 cup ground walnuts
- 1 stick butter, melted
- 3 tablespoons honey
- 1/2 teaspoon ground cardamom
- 1/2 teaspoon ground cinnamon
- Filling:
- 24 ounces cream cheese, at room temperature
- 8 ounces Greek-style yogurt
- 1 cup granulated sugar
- 1 teaspoon vanilla paste
- 3 extra-large eggs, at room temperature

Directions:

1. Select the "Air Fry" function and adjust the temperature to 400 degrees F. Press the "Start" key.
2. Mix all the crust ingredients; press the crust into a baking pan. Bake the crust for 6 minutes and allow it to cool on wire racks.
3. Using an electric mixer, whip the cream cheese, yogurt, granulated sugar, and vanilla paste until fluffy; add one egg at a time and continue to beat until creamy.
4. Pour the filling mixture onto the crust. Bake your cheesecake at 390 degrees F for 15 minutes.
5. Allow your cheesecake to cool completely before serving. Enjoy!

Nutrition:

- Info437 Calories,34.3g Fat,22.5g Carbs,10.4g Protei.

Easy Vanilla Donuts

Servings: 8
Cooking Time: 20 Minutes
Ingredients:

- 1 package refrigerated buttermilk biscuits
- 2 tablespoons butter, melted
- Vanilla glaze:
- 1 cup powdered sugar
- 2 ounces coconut milk
- 1 teaspoon pure vanilla extract

Directions:

1. Separate the biscuits and cut holes out of the center of each biscuit using a 1-inch round biscuit cutter; place them on parchment paper. Brush them with melted butter.

2. Select the "Air Fry" function and adjust the temperature to 350 degrees F. Press the "Start" key.

3. Lower your biscuits into the baking pan.

4. Air fry your biscuits at 340 degrees F for about 15 minutes or until golden brown, flipping them halfway through the cooking time.

5. Meanwhile, in a medium bowl, whisk together the powdered sugar, milk, and vanilla until smooth and creamy.

6. Dip the warm donuts into the vanilla glaze and enjoy!

Nutrition:

- Info222 Calories,8.4g Fat,31.7g Carbs,2.4g Protei.

Walnut Banana Bread

Servings: 7
Cooking Time: 20 Minutes
Ingredients:

- 2 cups all-purpose flour
- 1/2 cups ground walnuts
- 1 teaspoon baking powder
- 1 teaspoon baking soda
- 1/4 teaspoon kosher salt
- 1 stick butter, melted
- 1 cup brown sugar
- 2 ounces agave nectar
- 2 large eggs, whisked
- 4 medium ripe bananas, mashed
- 1/2 cup buttermilk

Directions:

1. Brush a baking pan with a nonstick cooking spray oil; set it aside.

2. Mix the dry ingredients; thoroughly combine the wet ingredients. Add the wet mixture to the dry mixture and mix until everything is well incorporated.

3. Select the "Bake" function and adjust the temperature to 330 degrees F. Press the "Start" key. When the display indicates "Add Food", place the baking pan on the air fryer tray.

4. Bake the banana bread for 15 minutes or until a tester comes out clean when inserted in the middle.

5. Bon appétit!

Nutrition:

- Info432 Calories,18.8g Fat,59.5g Carbs,7.8g Protei.

Vanilla Oatmeal Bars

Servings: 7
Cooking Time: 25 Minutes
Ingredients:

- 1 cup whole wheat flour
- 1 cups old-fashioned oats
- 1/2 teaspoon baking powder
- 1/2 teaspoon baking soda
- 1 stick butter, melted
- 1/2 cup brown sugar
- 2 medium eggs, beaten
- 1 teaspoon vanilla paste
- 1/4 teaspoon sea salt

Directions:

1. Select the "Air Fry" function and adjust the temperature to 360 degrees F. Press the "Start" key.

2. In a large mixing bowl, stir together all the dry ingredients. In another bowl, mix the wet ingredients.

3. Add the wet mixture to the dry ingredients and stir to combine well.

4. Press the batter onto a parchment-lined baking pan. Bake the oatmeal bars for approximately 15 minutes or until golden brown.

5. Let it sit on a wire rack for 20 minutes before slicing and serving.

6. Bon appétit!

Nutrition:

- Info306 Calories,16.2g Fat,34.4g Carbs,7.6g Protei.

Halloween Pumpkin Cupcakes

Servings: 6
Cooking Time: 20 Minutes
Ingredients:
- 1 ½ cups all-purpose flour
- 1 teaspoon baking powder
- 1/2 teaspoon baking powder
- A pinch of sea salt
- 1 teaspoon pumpkin spice mix
- 1/4 cup butter, at room temperature
- 1/2 cup brown sugar
- 2 eggs, beaten
- 1 cup pumpkin puree

Directions:
1. Line a muffin tin with parchment paper and set it aside.
2. Mix the dry ingredients, then, thoroughly combine the wet ingredients. Add the wet mixture to the dry mixture and mix until everything is well incorporated. Fold in the berries.
3. Select the "Bake" function and adjust the temperature to 330 degrees F. Press the "Start" key. When the display indicates "Add Food", place the muffin tin on the air fryer tray.
4. Bake the cupcakes for 15 minutes or until a tester comes out clean when inserted in the middle.
5. Bon appétit!
Nutrition:
- Info287 Calories,9.5g Fat,45.4g Carbs,5.6g Protei.

Sweet Cinnamon Almonds

Servings: 6
Cooking Time: 10 Minutes
Ingredients:
- 1 ½ cups raw almonds
- 2 tablespoons salted butter, melted
- 2 tablespoons brown sugar
- 1/2 teaspoon ground cinnamon

Directions:
1. Select the "Roast" function and adjust the temperature to 320 degrees F. Press the "Start" key.
2. In a mixing dish, toss all the ingredients.
3. When the display indicates "Add Food", place the almonds in the air fryer oven pan.
4. Roast your almonds in the preheated air fryer for 8 minutes, tossing them halfway through the cooking time to ensure even cooking.
5. Bon appétit!
Nutrition:
- Info242 Calories,20.4g Fat,10.5g Carbs,7.7g Protei.

Homemade Pâte à Choux

Servings: 6
Cooking Time: 1 Hour 20 Minutes
Ingredients:
- 2 tablespoons coconut oil, melted
- 2 tablespoons aquafaba
- 1 teaspoon vanilla extract
- 3 cups all-purpose flour
- 1/4 teaspoon ground cinnamon

Directions:
1. Select the "Air Fry" function and adjust the temperature to 360 degrees F. Press the "Start" key.
2. Using the paddle attachment, thoroughly combine the coconut oil, aquafaba, and vanilla. Now, slowly and gradually, add in the flour and cinnamon.
3. Knead the dough for approximately 3 minutes; cover the dough with a clean dish towel and let it rise for 1 hour in a warm place.
4. Roll out the dough and cut it into 24 squares.
5. Select the "Air Fry" function and adjust the temperature to 350 degrees F. Press the "Start" key.
6. Lower the squares into a lightly greased baking pan.
7. Air fry the squares at 340 degrees F for about 15 minutes or until golden brown, flipping them halfway through the cooking time.
8. Serve with toppings of choice and enjoy!
Nutrition:
- Info269 Calories,5.2g Fat,47.9g Carbs,6.5g Protei.

Classic French Toast With Honey

Servings: 4
Cooking Time: 15 Minutes
Ingredients:
- 2 eggs, beaten
- 2 tablespoons half-and-half
- 1/2 teaspoons ground cinnamon
- 1/4 teaspoons ground cardamom
- 1/2 teaspoon vanilla extract
- 1 loaf challah bread, cut into thick slices
- 4 tablespoons honey

Directions:
1. Select the "air fryer" function and adjust the temperature to 390 degrees F. Press the "Start" key.
2. In a mixing dish, whisk the eggs, half-and-half, cinnamon, cardamom, and vanilla extract.
3. Dip all the slices of challah bread in this mixture.
4. When the display indicates "Add Food", place the French toast in the air fryer oven pan.
5. Bake in the preheated air fryer for 10 minutes, turning them over halfway through the cooking time to ensure even cooking.
6. Drizzle your French toast with honey and enjoy!
Nutrition:
- Info412 Calories,6.2g Fat,75.2g Carbs,13.1g Protei.

Decadent Brownie With Sultanas

Servings: 8
Cooking Time: 20 Minutes
Ingredients:

- 1 cup all-purpose flour
- 1 cup unsweetened cocoa powder
- 1/3 cup butter
- 2 ounces dark chocolate
- 2 ounces Sultanas
- 1 cup sugar
- A pinch of salt
- A pinch of grated nutmeg
- 2 eggs, beaten
- 1 teaspoon vanilla paste
- 1/4 teaspoon ground anise

Directions:

1. Brush a baking pan with nonstick cooking spray oil; set it aside.
2. Mix the dry ingredients; now, thoroughly combine the wet ingredients. Add the wet mixture to the dry mixture and mix until everything is well incorporated.
3. Select the "Bake" function and adjust the temperature to 330 degrees F. Press the "Start" key. When the display indicates "Add Food", place the baking pan on the air fryer tray.
4. Bake your brownie for 15 minutes or until a tester comes out clean when inserted in the middle.
5. Bon appétit!

Nutrition:

- Info277 Calories,13.3g Fat,39.7g Carbs,5.9g Protei.

Peach Crumble Cake

Servings: 6
Cooking Time: 15 Minutes
Ingredients:

- 1/2 cup old-fashioned oats
- 1/4 cup almond meal
- 1/2 teaspoon baking powder
- A pinch of sea salt
- 1/4 cup butter, cold
- 3 large peaches, peeled, pitted and diced
- 1/2 teaspoon ground anise
- 1 teaspoon ginger, peeled and ground
- 1 teaspoon ground cinnamon
- 1/4 cup brown sugar
- 1 tablespoon honey

Directions:

1. Select the "Bake" function and adjust the temperature to 360 degrees F. Press the "Start" key.
2. Mix the oats, almond meal, baking powder, salt, and butter. Mix until smooth and uniform.
3. Press the mixture into a lightly greased baking pan. Toss the peaches with the remaining ingredients and place them on the crust.
4. Bake the crumble cake for approximately 12 minutes or until the topping is golden brown. Enjoy!

Nutrition:

- Info227 Calories,10.8g Fat,25.4g Carbs,4g Protei.

Apple Almond Crisp

Servings: 8
Cooking Time: 20 Minutes
Ingredients:

- 2 large apples, peeled, cored and diced
- 1/2 teaspoon ground cardamom
- 1/2 teaspoon ground cinnamon
- 1/4 teaspoon ground nutmeg
- 2 tablespoons almonds, slivered
- Topping:
- 1/2 cup all-purpose flour
- 1/2 cup almond meal
- 1/2 teaspoon baking powder
- 1/4 teaspoon sea salt
- 1/2 cup brown sugar
- 2 eggs, beaten
- 1/2 cup coconut oil

Directions:

1. Select the "Air Fry" function and adjust the temperature to 360 degrees F. Press the "Start" key.
2. Toss the apples with cardamom, cinnamon, nutmeg, and almonds in a lightly greased baking pan.
3. Mix the flour, almond meal, baking powder, salt, and sugar in a bowl. Then, stir in the eggs and coconut oil. Mix until smooth and uniform.
4. Drop tablespoons of the batter onto the fruit layer. Lower the pan onto the air fryer tray and bake your crisp for approximately 12 minutes or until the apples are bubbly and the topping is golden brown.
5. Bon appétit!

Nutrition:

- Info258 Calories,18.4g Fat,21.7g Carbs,3.8g Protei.

Coconut And Blueberry Cookie Cups

Servings: 6
Cooking Time: 20 Minutes
Ingredients:

- 1 egg
- 1/2 cup coconut sugar
- 1/4 cup coconut oil
- 4 tablespoons coconut milk
- 1/2 teaspoon pure vanilla extract
- 1 teaspoon crystallized ginger
- 1/2 teaspoon ground cinnamon
- 1/2 cup all-purpose flour
- 1/2 cup coconut flour
- 1/2 teaspoon baking powder
- A pinch of kosher salt
- 1/2 cup blueberries

Directions:

1. Brush a muffin tin with nonstick cooking spray oil; set it aside.
2. Mix the dry ingredients, then, thoroughly combine the wet ingredients. Add the wet mixture to the dry mixture and mix until everything is well incorporated. Fold in the berries.
3. Select the "Bake" function and adjust the temperature to 330 degrees F. Press the "Start" key. When the display indicates "Add Food", place the baking pan on the air fryer tray.
4. Bake the cookie cups for 15 minutes or until a tester comes out clean when inserted in the middle.
5. Bon appétit!

Nutrition:

- Info311 Calories,19.9g Fat,29.8g Carbs,4.7g Protei.

Classic Cinnamon Tostada

Servings: 2
Cooking Time: 10 Minutes
Ingredients:

- 2 whole-wheat tortillas, cut into triangles
- 2 tablespoons brown sugar
- 1 teaspoon ground cinnamon
- 2 tablespoons butter, softened

Directions:

1. Select the "air fryer" function and adjust the temperature to 390 degrees F. Press the "Start" key.
2. Toss the tortilla chunks with the remaining ingredients.
3. When the display indicates "Add Food", place the French toast in the air fryer oven pan.
4. Bake in the preheated air fryer for 8 minutes, turning them over halfway through the cooking time to ensure even cooking.
5. Enjoy!
Nutrition:

- Info296 Calories,14.3g Fat,38.5g Carbs,4g Protei.

Golden Banana Bites

Servings: 3
Cooking Time: 15 Minutes
Ingredients:

- 1 large egg, beaten
- 1/2 cup rice flour
- 1/2 cup breadcrumbs
- 1/2 teaspoon ground cinnamon
- 1/4 teaspoon grated nutmeg
- 1/4 teaspoon ground cloves
- 2 tablespoons coconut sugar
- 2 medium bananas, peeled and sliced

Directions:

1. Select the "Air Fry" function and adjust the temperature to 350 degrees F. Press the "Start" key.
2. In a mixing dish, thoroughly combine the egg and rice flour. In a separate bowl, mix the remaining ingredients until well combined.
3. Dredge each slice of banana into the flour mixture. Then, roll them over the breadcrumb mixture.
4. Bake the banana slices in the preheated air fryer for approximately 10 minutes, flipping them halfway through the cooking time. Bon appétit!

Nutrition:

- Info234 Calories,2.6g Fat,48.4g Carbs,50.2g Protei.

Churros With Chocolate Syrup

Servings: 2
Cooking Time: 10 Minutes
Ingredients:

- 2 frozen waffles
- 1/3 cup coconut cream
- 1/4 cup maple syrup
- 2 tablespoons cocoa powder
- 1/4 cup chocolate chips

Directions:

1. Select the "Air Fry" function and adjust the temperature to 350 degrees F. Press the "Start" key.
2. Air fry the waffles for about 3 minutes. Flip the waffles and continue to cook for 3 minutes.
3. In a mixing bowl, thoroughly combine all the remaining ingredients to prepare the chocolate syrup; microwave the chocolate syrup for 30 seconds.
4. Serve your waffles with the chocolate syrup on the side.
5. Enjoy!
Nutrition:

- Info420 Calories,23.2g Fat,52.2g Carbs,5.7g Protei.

Baked Apples With Walnuts And Raisins

Servings: 4
Cooking Time: 20 Minutes
Ingredients:

- 4 large apples
- 1/2 cup old-fashioned rolled oats
- 1/4 cup walnuts, chopped
- 2 tablespoons coconut oil
- 1/4 cup brown sugar
- 1/2 teaspoon ground cardamom
- 1/2 teaspoon ground cinnamon
- 1/4 teaspoon ground nutmeg
- 1/8 teaspoon kosher salt
- 2 tablespoons raisins

Directions:

1. Use a paring knife to remove the stem and seeds from the apples, making deep holes.
2. In a mixing bowl, thoroughly combine the remaining ingredients. Divide the filling between the apples.
3. Select the "Air Fry" function and adjust the temperature to 350 degrees F. Press the "Start" key.
4. Bake the apples for 12 minutes and serve at room temperature. Enjoy!

Nutrition:

- Info307 Calories,11.2g Fat,57.2g Carbs,3.6g Protei.

Classic Banana Bread

Servings: 6
Cooking Time: 20 Minutes
Ingredients:

- 3 overripe bananas, peeled and mashed
- 1/2 cup self-raising flour
- 1 teaspoon baking powder
- 3 medium eggs, at room temperature
- 1/2 cup granulated sugar
- 1/2 cup coconut oil, melted
- 1/4 teaspoon ground cardamom
- 1/2 teaspoon ground cinnamon

Directions:

1. Brush a baking pan with nonstick cooking spray oil; set it aside.
2. Mix the dry ingredients; thoroughly combine the wet ingredients. Add the wet mixture to the dry mixture and mix until everything is well incorporated.
3. Select the "Bake" function and adjust the temperature to 330 degrees F. Press the "Start" key.
When the display indicates "Add Food", place the baking pan on the air fryer tray.
4. Bake your banana bread for 15 minutes or until a tester comes out clean when inserted in the middle.
5. Bon appétit!

Nutrition:

- Info312 Calories,20.5g Fat,29.7g Carbs,4.5g Protei.

Greek-style Banana Cake

Servings: 6
Cooking Time: 20 Minutes
Ingredients:

- 3/4 cup cake flour
- 3/4 cup caster sugar
- 1/2 cup butter, melted
- 2 medium eggs, beaten
- 1/2 teaspoon almond extract
- 1/2 teaspoon vanilla extract
- 1/4 teaspoon ground cardamom
- 1/3 teaspoon crystallized ginger
- 1/4 cup Greek-style yogurt
- 2 overripe bananas, peeled and mashed

Directions:

1. Brush a baking pan with a nonstick cooking spray oil; set it aside.
2. Mix the dry ingredients; thoroughly combine the wet ingredients. Add the wet mixture to the dry mixture and mix until everything is well incorporated.
3. Select the "Bake" function and adjust the temperature to 330 degrees F. Press the "Start" key. When the display indicates "Add Food", place the baking pan on the air fryer tray.
4. Bake banana bread for 15 minutes or until a tester comes out clean when inserted in the middle.
5. Bon appétit!

Nutrition:

- Info359 Calories,17.1g Fat,48.4g Carbs,4.8g Protei.

Mini Banana Muffins

Servings: 6
Cooking Time: 20 Minutes
Ingredients:

- 1 cup all-purpose flour
- 1/2 cup walnuts, ground
- 1/2 teaspoon baking powder
- 1 teaspoon baking soda
- 1/4 teaspoon kosher salt
- 3 large overripe bananas, mashed
- 1/2 cup granulated sugar
- 2 tablespoons honey
- 2 eggs, beaten
- 1/2 cup coconut oil

Directions:

1. Brush a muffin tin with a nonstick cooking spray oil; set it aside.
2. Mix the dry ingredients; thoroughly combine the wet ingredients. Add the wet mixture to the dry mixture and mix until everything is well incorporated.
3. Select the "Bake" function and adjust the temperature to 330 degrees F. Press the "Start" key. When the display indicates "Add Food", place the baking pan on the air fryer tray.
4. Bake the mini banana muffins for 15 minutes or until a tester comes out clean when inserted in the middle.
5. Bon appétit!

Nutrition:

- Info411 Calories,24.3g Fat,46.5g Carbs,5.7g Protei.

Apple Maple Cups

Servings: 4
Cooking Time: 15 Minutes
Ingredients:

- 2 large apples, peeled, cored, and diced
- 4 tablespoons granulated sugar
- 1/2 teaspoon ground cinnamon
- 1/2 teaspoon ground cardamom
- 1/2 teaspoon ginger, peeled and minced
- Topping:
- 1 cup all-purpose flour
- 1 cup old-fashioned oats
- 1/2 cup brown sugar
- 2 tablespoons maple syrup
- 1 teaspoon ground cinnamon
- 1/4 teaspoon grated nutmeg
- 1/8 teaspoon kosher salt
- 1/2 stick butter

Directions:

1. Grease ramekins with a nonstick cooking spray and set them aside.
2. Select the "Air Fry" function and adjust the temperature to 360 degrees F. Press the "Start" key.
3. Toss the apples with granulated sugar, cinnamon, cardamom, and ginger; divide the mixture between ramekins.
4. Mix the flour, oats, sugar, maple syrup, cinnamon, nutmeg, salt, and butter in a bowl. Mix until smooth and uniform.
5. Drop tablespoons of the batter onto the fruit layer.
6. Bake the apple cups for approximately 12 minutes or until the topping is golden brown.
7. Bon appétit!

Nutrition:

- Info494 Calories,14.6g Fat,85.9g Carbs,8.5g Protei.

RECIPES INDEX

Classic Breakfast Frittata 16

Classic Breakfast Pancakes 15

Classic Cauliflower Steaks 36

Classic Chicken Cutlets 43

Classic Cinnamon Tostada 93

Classic Festive Turkey 46

Classic French Toast With Honey 91

Classic Fried Sea Scallops 53

Classic Fried Tofu 34

Classic Lentil Meatballs 35

Classic Mini Cheesecakes 87

Classic Pork Burgers 72

Classic Porterhouse Steaks 75

Classic Tortilla Chips 79

Coconut And Blueberry Cookie Cups 93

Coconut Fried Banana 23

Corn And Zucchini Fritters 17

Country-style Apple Oatmeal Fritters 80

Creamed Chicken Salad 48

Creamy Turkey Salad 50

Creole Catfish Fillets 60

Crispy Breaded Mushrooms 36

Crispy Codfish Fillets 54

Crispy Pork Tenderloin 77

Crunch-crunch Party Mix 21

Curried Chicken Cups 50

D

Decadent Bourbon Carrots 38

Decadent Brownie With Sultanas 92

Dijon Feta Broccoli 33

Dijon Pork Chops 78

Double Cheese Breakfast Casserole 15

E

Easy Apple Crumble 89

Easy Bacon Cups 15

Easy Breakfast Granola 85

Easy Cinnamon Donuts 83

Easy Fried Tempeh 41

Easy Greek Kolokythokeftéthes 79

Easy Roasted Asparagus 30

Easy Scotch Fillets 69

Easy Vanilla Donuts 90

Egg In A Hole 14

Entrecôte Steak With Cauliflower 70

F

Father's Day Croissants 88

Favorite Pork Salad 62

Favorite Seafood Fritters 58

Favorite Seafood Sliders 57

Favorite Turkey Meatballs 44

Festive Baked Ham 66

Festive Chicken Rolls 44

Festive Pork Butt 76

Fish Salad Sandwich 56

French-style Roasted Parsnip 32

Fried Bacon Slices 12

Fried Banana Slices 87

Fried Broccoli Florets 41

Fried Green Beans 39

Fried Tofu With Sweet Potatoes 35

G

Garlic Parmesan Chicken Wings 49

Garlicky Butter Turkey 45

Garlicky Flounder Fillets 60

Giant Dutch Pancake 11

Golden Banana Bites 93

Gorgonzola Paprika Drumettes 20

Grandma's Baked Apples 88

Grandma's Chicken Roulade 45

Grandma's Roasted Squash 32

Greek Pita Wraps 82

Greek-style Banana Cake 94

Greek-style Cheesecake 89

Greek-style Eggplant 28

Printed in Great Britain
by Amazon

21778064R00057